...... dramatic accounts of how God was moving among the people of that country. Later, as a young evangelist, God renewed my burden for India as I prayed with Mark Buntain on the streets of Calcutta. He would later be known as "St. Mark of Calcutta" because of building the great Mission of Mercy hospital and ministry that would become known worldwide. Even Mother Teresa ministered there on occasion.

I share that to express firsthand my understanding of Dr. Charles Doss' burden for India and the excitement of God's miracle-working power there and throughout the Earth. I have known him now for many years and can say with assurance that the details of God's moving in his life will inspire you. A burning desire to see the lost reached for Christ is at the heart of his ministry, as it is of mine, and it is my hope that this book will spark that same desire in you. May the Holy Spirit fan that spark into a flame for souls that would reproduce results like those you'll read of in this book, *Led by the Master's Hand.*

Tommy Barnett
Pastor, Phoenix First Assembly of God Church

The highest compliment that we can give God is the testimony of our lives changed for His glory. In Brother Doss' *Led by the Master's Hand*, he takes the reader on an exciting journey around the world as he allows us to witness God's constant miraculous provision. Whether one is a new believer or a seasoned minister, reading about the life story of Brother Doss, as he was called to evangelize the outer parts of the Earth, will inspire you to reach out to God and believe Him to perform mighty miracles today in your life.

Bob Weiner
Bob & Rose Weiner Ministries International
Gainesville, Florida

You will be blessed by the testimony of this man of faith. When Brother Charles Doss came to Hong Kong in 1963, he brought two things: the power of God and a great love for souls. He had received this anointing through prayer and fasting.

We had mighty outpourings of the Holy Spirit in every meeting, and the lives of many Chinese, both Christians and non-Christians, were changed. The impact of this ministry has lasted to this day. I can honestly say that Charles Doss is a true revivalist sent from God.

Gwen R. Shaw
Missionary to China, 1947-1978
Founder & President, End-Time Handmaidens

Rev. Charles Doss and his ministry have been a source of challenge and inspiration to my life since I first met him in 1966. That year he held the first of a number of powerful revivals at my father's church in Richmond, Virginia, where miracles and signs and wonders followed his preaching of the Word of God. His heart for the nations of the world and his willingness to pour himself out for the multitudes continues until this day. I love the way he walks in a simplicity of faith that produces great results.

Ruth Ward Heflin
Ashland, Virginia

I have been closely associated with Dr. Charles W. Doss from the year 1967. The Lord has been using him in an exceptional way. I have seen with my very eyes miracles take place as he ministered to the needy people. His heart of compassion attracted me towards this humble servant of God more than anything else. I still cherish the love and affection he showered on me while I was very sick in the U.S.A. in the year 1985.

There is no doubt that this book, *Led by the Master's Hand*, will be a source of inspiration to thousands of people worldwide. I pray that the Almighty God will make it a great blessing to all those who read it.

Dr. D. G. S. Dhinakaran
Jesus Calls Ministries
Madras, South India

What a delight it is to endorse the gifting of a man of God who is able to sing his testimony into the hearts of thousands of people! *Led by the Master's Hand* is the life story of Brother Charles Doss as he has been prompted, led and released by the love of Almighty God. This book is a testimony of God's miraculous provision and abundant grace to anyone who is willing to trust in the Lord.

Dr. Joy Seevaratnam, MD
Senior Pastor, Full Gospel Assembly
Penang, Malaysia

Led by the
Master's
Hand

Missionary Journeys of
Signs, Wonders and Miracles

by

Charles W. Doss

McDougal Publishing is a division of The McDougal Foundation, Inc., a Maryland nonprofit corporation dedicated to spreading the Gospel of the Lord Jesus Christ to as many people as possible in the shortest time possible.

Published by:

McDougal Publishing
P.O. Box 3595
Hagerstown, MD 21742-3595

Second Edition

ISBN 1-884369-48-0
(Previously ISBN 1-880728-00-1)

Printed in the United States of America
For Worldwide Distribution

DEDICATION

I dedicate this book to my beloved wife Grace and my three sons, Alexander William, Joshua James and Elijah Paul.

May the Lord bless them for their dedication and sacrifice, especially for their patience during the time I am away from them on my missionary journeys.

Their prayers and encouragement have been a great blessing to me in my ministry. My prayer is that our three sons would rise up to be mighty warriors for the King of kings and the Lord of lords, our Lord Jesus Christ.

ACKNOWLEDGMENTS

I wish to give special acknowledgment to Mona Carter, our dear sister in the Lord, for her tireless service in spending many, many hours typing this book for the printing.

I would also like to thank Mary Lou Sather for her careful editing of the manuscript.

They have done all this solely for the glory of God. May the Lord bless them and their families.

CONTENTS

FOREWORD
BY GERALD DERSTINE

For more than thirty-seven years, I have followed the life of Missionary Evangelist Charles W. Doss. It is obvious that a very special anointing of God's grace and power accompanies this brother's life, and there is no doubt that this book, *Led by the Master's Hand,* will be a classic to inspire, instruct and motivate many ministers and leaders in God's Kingdom. Brother Doss has a God-given style of preaching, which is also manifest in his writing.

Your faith will certainly be charged up by this book. Allow the miracles and biblical instructions you read to stimulate your life, and then share the contents of this book with others. God will use you, even as He did Brother Doss.

There is a need for testimonial (personal experience) books today. A new army of ministers and leaders is being raised up in our world to carry the torch of the Gospel. This book will be used as one of God's instruments for this purpose.

Dr. Gerald G. Derstine
Chairman, Gospel Crusade, Inc.
Director, Christian Retreat
Bradenton, Florida

INTRODUCTION

The globe of the world that had been circling above me suddenly came to rest on my shoulders. I had gathered with about thirty of my friends to pray for a special weekend meeting in England, and while we prayed this unusual manifestation came. *What could it mean?* I wondered. With deep concern, I asked the Lord to reveal to me the meaning of the circling globe.

Just then the other members of the group gathered in a circle around me, and a Scottish evangelist who was praying with us laid his hands on me and began to prophesy. He said that I would be in the middle of a very large crowd of dark-skinned people, reaping the harvest for Christ.

Although the evangelist said many other wonderful things, my mind was strongly directed to those words "reaping the harvest for Christ." I suddenly realized that the globe resting on my shoulders was a burden that was being placed on me for the souls of humanity worldwide, and I took it as a solemn command from the Lord to evangelize the world. From that moment on, a burden for souls has been very heavy on my heart.

I immediately began a thirty-day fast, seeking the Lord for His direction and His wisdom. I was so serious about it that I locked myself in my room, seeking to hear from Heaven. On the final day of my fast I heard an audible voice, directing me to go to Kingston, Jamaica.

I did not know a single soul in the West Indies who could invite me or house me or support me financially.

The journey to Jamaica was taken by total faith in God's leading and in His providence. Like Abraham, *"when he was called to go out into a place," "obeyed,"* and *"went out, not knowing whither [where] he went"* (Hebrews 11:8), I, too, took a journey of faith, and the results were astounding. The Lord Himself went with me, and confirmed the preaching and teaching of His Word with signs following, as He promised (see Mark 16:20).

The journey to Jamaica was my first missionary journey, but ever since that time, I have been *Led by the Master's Hand* to many other parts of the world to reap the whitened harvest for the Kingdom of God. My goal is to reach at least one million souls for Christ before His return, and so far more than nine hundred thousand souls have been ushered into His kingdom through this ministry.

This book is written to declare the wonders of God's providence and of His leading and guidance, and to encourage every born-again believer to get involved in evangelism, the heartbeat of God. He who has called you to this work is faithful and He will supply all your need *"according to his riches in glory by Christ Jesus"* (Philippians 4:19). We do not depend on our own faith, but on God's faithfulness to keep all of His precious promises. He has declared:

> *My covenant will I not break, nor alter the thing that is gone out of my lips.* Psalm 89:34

Dr. Charles Doss
Scottsdale, Arizona

CHAPTER 1

THE EARLY YEARS

He brought me up also out of an horrible pit, out of the miry clay, and set my feet upon a rock, and established my goings. Psalm 40:2

From my birth, in Madras, South India, I was a very sickly child. My childhood memories are filled with suffering — from epilepsy, kidney problems, a blood disorder and many other illnesses which caused me great misery. I was isolated and under uninterrupted care, both in hospitals and at home. Loneliness was my constant companion. If I wanted to do anything or go anywhere, I had to have a servant or a family member with me, and I was unable to play with other children. On the few occasions I tried to climb trees, as other boys did, I would have an epileptic seizure. Void of social acceptance, I was overwhelmed by rejection, fear and utter frustration.

My father was a government official during the British occupation, and we lived a comfortable life because of his position. My parents tried everything the medical profession could offer to restore my health, but to no avail. I was in and out of hospitals constantly. The government permitted a small private hospital to be built near our bungalow just for the families of government officials. This hospital became, in a sense, my home. Despite all the special care and the nutritious foods I ate, I grew progressively thinner.

My grandmother came to stay with us now and then and took care of me whenever she could. Her favorite treatment for me was cod liver oil, which she administered both internally and externally. Early in the morning, at sunrise, she would pray and then she would rub my body with the cod liver oil. My skinny body would be smothered in the oil so that I smelled like a fish. I was grateful to all those who were doing their best to help me, but despite their best efforts, my health went from bad to worse, and I became bitter.

One evening, when I was ten, my body abruptly began to swell, and I seemed to be at the point of death. We were nominal Christians, Anglicans (Church of England), and in the middle of that night, my mother began to cry out to God to preserve my life. Since it was so late, the only thing she could do was call our rickshaw man and rush me to the hospital.

When we arrived at the hospital, no doctors and no emergency services were available because it was so late. The only person on duty was a nurse's aide, and she advised my mother to come back the next day.

My mother did not know what to do. As she sat in the rickshaw, holding me across her lap and weeping helplessly, a tall, distinguished-looking gentleman approached us from across the grounds. He introduced himself as a doctor and asked my mother why she was crying. He told her that he ordinarily had no reason for coming to the hospital at that late hour, but something had drawn him to take a walk in the area. After my mother told him of my condition, he realized the reason for his coming. He instructed my mother to take me to his house immediately. He discovered that I had kidney failure, and he began treatment right away, saving my life. God's remarkable provision had sent a kidney specialist to meet my specific need.

Though my life had been spared from kidney failure, I continued to suffer from other maladies. The attacks of epilepsy from which I had long suffered brought great heartache to our family. My many infirmities kept me from gaining weight, and I looked like a walking corpse. On the eve of my fourteenth birthday, I had massive epileptic attacks, one after another. My father, who was a very strong man emotionally and had never broken down and cried easily, was reduced to tears of grief. For years his prayer had been that God would heal me, but his desperation led him to wish that everything would end for me that night.

The next day, on my fourteenth birthday, when every human effort had failed, the Lord visited me. As I lay in bed, the Lord Jesus stepped into my room and changed the gloomy atmosphere into His glory. As the beloved song says, "Heaven came down and glory filled my soul." [1] It was like the words of another great song:

> *When Jesus comes, the tempter's power is broken,*
> *When Jesus comes, the tears are wiped away.*
> *He breaks the gloom and fills the life with glory*
> *That all may change when Jesus comes to stay.* [2]

Led by the Master's Hand

Jesus raised me up from my deathbed, with complete deliverance from every ailment I had suffered. I was instantly and completely healed.

Since the Master's touch came to me on that very special birthday, I have never suffered any serious illness. Instead, I have grown stronger and stronger in the strength of the Lion of Judah. Surely God had His hand on me for some special purpose. Hallelujah!

1. "Heaven Came Down and Glory Filled My Soul" by John W. Peterson. Copyright © 1961 by Singspiration, Inc.
2. "Then Jesus Comes" by Oswald J. Smith & Homer Rodeheaver. Copyright © 1940 by The Rodeheaver Company.

Chapter 2

From Madras to Swansea

Then the word of the Lord came unto me, saying, Before I formed thee in the belly I knew thee; and before thou camest forth out of the womb I sanctified thee, and I ordained thee a prophet unto the nations.

Jeremiah 1:4-5

I was now healthy, and my next question was, "What do I want to do with my life?" Because of my many illnesses, I had not attended school regularly, nor had I learned the important self-discipline that a regular education would have taught me. I tried going to school with others my age, but I was unable to fix my mind on my schoolwork. My father was very concerned and felt that perhaps a trade would be better suited to me, so I attended several different trade schools. When that didn't work, I tried the military. I went from one thing to another, and found, to my dismay, that I was unsuccessful at everything I put my hand to.

I had studied music a bit and began to spend much of my time playing my guitar. I seemed to have an aptitude for music, and the thought came to me that perhaps I could be a jazz guitarist and travel the world. My father was not very happy about this prospect, but because

I had failed in everything else and he was at a loss to know what to advise me, he allowed me to go abroad to seek my life.

In time, I found myself living in Swansea, South Wales, and there I began to frequent a popular night spot called "Mumble's Pier." It was a place that featured juke-boxes, pinball and game machines, and a dance floor. One night, as I sat dropping coins into the jukebox, a girl sat nearby listening to the songs I was playing. She remarked that I was playing all her favorite tunes and was surprised that our musical tastes were so similar. "My name is Mary Williams," she said. "Where are you from?"

"I am from Madras, India," I replied politely.

"Oh," said Mary enthusiastically, "Would you like to come and meet my father? He's a pastor, and he really likes international students." So I went with Mary to her home and met her father.

Mary was right. Her father was very kind to me. "Are you a Christian?" he asked me.

"Yes, I am," I replied. As I said, we were nominal Christians, but we were not Hindus or Buddhists or Moslems or Zoroastrians or followers of one of the many of the other faiths of India, so we were considered to be "Christians." Like many, I had grown up thinking that the only thing necessary to be a Christian was to have your name on the rolls of a Christian church.

Pastor Williams' next question surprised me: "Would you like to be a *good* Christian?"

This was something to ponder. I went to church some-times, and I believed in God and in Jesus Christ. At least I believed that they existed. Yet I was keenly aware that throughout my boyhood I had not demonstrated any Christian virtues. I was mischievous, always getting into trouble, and my mother often told me that I would never get to Heaven if I did not mend my ways. Perhaps this pastor knew something I needed to know. Would I like to be a *good* Christian? What was he talking about?

Pastor Williams carefully explained to me how to be "born again," as he called it. When he said this, I was just as confused as Nicodemus had been when Jesus told him the same thing (see John chapter 3). To be polite, I listened carefully to what he was saying, and when he asked me to pray a prayer of repentance, I did so. I just wanted to get out of there as soon as possible because Mary and I were planning to go to the movies that evening, and I did not want to miss a treat like that.

As Pastor Williams came to know me better and see my interest in music, he said to me one day, "Charles, there is a church near here that has a wonderful music program. I am sure you would enjoy it immensely. Please let me show you the place." He took me to Spring Terrace Assemblies of God in Swansea and introduced me to Pastor Trevor Hewitt and his wife Muriel.

Discovering that I had very few resources, Pastor and Mrs. Hewitt invited me into their home, and I stayed with them for three months. While I was there, Muriel Hewitt taught me many Gospel songs, and I sang often at the services in the church. I was very polite to them all and pretended to be one of them, although I really still had no idea of how to change my life.

One evening Pastor Hewitt said, "Charles, you have been here for three months now, and we have never heard your testimony. Would you be willing to give your testimony at the meeting tonight?"

Now I was on the spot. He wanted me to give my testimony, and I had no testimony to give. I had nothing of which to testify. What should I do?

Embarrassed, I said I would rather sing — if that was all right with him. He agreed. The song I selected that evening was "Lord, Make Me a Channel of Blessing," [1] and as I sang, I found myself breaking down in tears, and then sobs. Quickly I finished singing and retreated to my usual seat in the back row of the sanctuary. For some reason, I was miserable.

As I sat there among those dear Christian brothers and sisters, I became more and more uncomfortable, until I began to have the sensation that I was sitting there stark naked. I could not understand why I should feel that way, for I had my usual Sunday clothes on. As I tried to push these thoughts from my mind, the Holy Spirit spoke to me and said, "You *are* naked in My sight, for you need the garment of righteousness. All these other people have clothed themselves in Me, but you have not. That is what you need."

I cried out, "Lord God, whatever it takes to cover my nakedness, do it!" and instantly my life was changed, and it was changed totally.

I was so excited that I wanted to dash home and sit alone in my room, just to savor the feeling that flooded me. I could not believe the difference I was experiencing.

One of the ladies said to me, "Charles, your face has a light in it that it never had before." I thought some of my hair tonic must have run onto my forehead and made my face shiny, so I put my hand up to wipe it off. "No! No!" she protested. "Charles, it is nothing on the outside. This is coming from within. Something has happened to you, hasn't it?"

She was right. Now I had a real testimony to give. Although I had prayed the prayer of repentance with Pastor Williams in an effort to be polite, it had taken more to make me realize my need of redemption. Pastor Williams had planted, Pastor Hewitt had watered and God had given the increase (see 1 Corinthians 3:6). That Sunday burns in my memory to this day.

A week before my conversion, I had sent off two letters. One was to apply for a job as a salesman, and the other, written on my behalf by Pastor Hewitt, was to inquire about entrance into the Bible College of Wales. Although I had not yet become a born-again believer, he felt in his spirit that God's hand was upon me for a great future ministry.

The day after my conversion I received answers to both of those letters. Early that morning, Pastor Hewitt came up to my room with the letters in his hand. He urged me to open the letter from the Bible College of Wales first.

The college had been founded in 1924 by Rees Howells, [2] a man of God who lived a remarkable life of faith. The college was known for its teaching on the life of faith. It was not founded with a committee, council, denomination or wealthy person behind it. No appeal was to be made for finances. One of the chief aims was to strengthen the faith of God's people by giving visible proof that He is the living and faithful God — Jehovah Jireh. [3]

As I read the letter, written by Dr. J.B. Simmons, senior tutor at the college, I strongly felt led to obey God's call. Dr. Simmons was enthusiastic about my coming. He, in fact, asked that I come immediately.

How strange! I had just been converted the previous night, and now I had an open door for preparation for the ministry.

But maybe it wasn't so strange. When Jesus called His disciples, He said, *"Follow me and I will make you fishers of men,"* and they immediately forsook their nets and followed Him. I knew that I needed to spend time at the Lord's feet and learn of Him. I quickly packed my few belongings, said good-bye to the Hewitts, and boarded a bus for the ten-minute ride from Swansea to the college.

When I arrived at the Bible College of Wales, I was interviewed by Dr. J.B. Simmons himself. The questions were simple, but to the point.

First he asked me when I had been saved. He must have been expecting to hear that I had been saved for several years, for he was startled when I told him that I had been saved the previous night.

Next he asked, "Do you believe, then, that Jesus has the power to save you?"

My reply was, "Definitely, yes."

The third question I did not understand very well: "Do you believe the Lord has the power to keep you?"

This time I was not so sure what I should answer. "Yeeesss," I answered quite hesitantly. Dr. Simmons went on to explain that the college was founded on the life of faith and that anyone who entered it was required to live that life. The training was not to be given free. Students at the college had to pay a considerable amount of money each term for their education, but they were not allowed to go out to earn money, nor were they allowed to solicit support from churches, relatives or friends. They had to look only to the Lord to supply all their needs: spiritual, physical and material. He wanted me to understand this clearly.

At the close of the interview, Dr. Simmons asked me if I was prepared to go ahead with my commitment. I knew, at this point, that I was launching out into the deep, just as the heroes of faith in the Bible had done. But I was willing and gave him a resounding "YES."

Dr. Simmons had one more question for me: "Do you have any money in your pocket now?"

As I searched through my pockets, I found just two pennies. He asked me to empty the contents of my pockets onto the desk, and he promptly took away my two pennies, telling me that I was now a fit candidate for the life of faith. He assured me that God Himself would now supply all my needs.

From that time on, it became my obligation to "pray through" until I received the money to pay my tuition every term and the resources to meet all my other needs. The rules concerning this obligation were rigidly observed.

During my first month in the college, the words of Jesus became my inspiration. He said:

If ye shall ask any thing in my name, I will do it.
John 14:14

I took His Word by faith and began to pray and ask Him for the money for my tuition. One day a miracle happened.

During our morning prayer meeting, all the staff and

students were present and, as usual, we were on our knees, praying for the needs of the college. I placed my Bible on my chair and knelt, leaning my chest against the Bible. My arms were under the chair; thus the Bible was between my chest and the chair. After a long period of prayer, we all rose from our knees. As I picked up my Bible, ten one-pound notes fell from under it.

This was the first time I had experienced a creative miracle, and it startled me. At first I thought someone might have put the money there. At the same time, I could not see how this could have happened without my knowledge, since I had been leaning against the Bible the entire time. I asked several of my friends on either side of me whether they had placed the money there. They assured me they had not, and they, too, were surprised at this concrete evidence of the Lord's gracious provision.

At the end of the meeting, I went to Dr. Simmons and told him about the money. He began to jump up and down with great joy. When he had calmed down enough to explain, he told me that God was sending angels to supply my needs directly from the Bank of Heaven. After this experience, I did not doubt God's keeping power. I was sure that what He promised was true:

For all the promises of God in him are yea, and in him Amen. 2 Corinthians 1:20

One of the well-known scripture phrases the college used often was *"Jehovah Jireh [the Lord will provide]"* (Genesis 22:14). God had promised that although Heaven and

24

Earth pass away, His Word would not fail. I began to realize how it pleases our heavenly Father when His children dare to believe Him and stand on His Word. He had said:

> *But without faith it is impossible to please him: for he that cometh to God must believe that he is, and that he is a rewarder of them that diligently seek him.*
>
> Hebrews 11:6

On many other occasions I experienced the provision of God in mysterious ways. Once, when I was scheduled to preach in the small village of Cowbridge, South Wales, I had no money for my bus fare. Still, I was required to go, so I was wondering what I would do.

I was supposed to leave with James, a fellow student, at 3:00 P.M., but when it came time to leave, I remained in my room. I didn't know what to do.

A few minutes before three there was a knock at the door, and James came in. "Are you ready to leave, Charles?" he asked.

"But, James," I said, "I have no money to go. Will you join me in prayer? Perhaps if we both pray, the money will come sooner."

"Charles! Look at the time!" he cried. "This is not the time to pray! It's time to go!" Turning, he marched out the door and headed for the bus stop. I followed, assuming from his confident manner that he had some money with him to take care of the fares.

Since it was Saturday, the bus was packed with young people. James and I were standing with many young people around us, when the conductress came to collect the fares. She first turned to James. He looked at me, for he also did not have a single penny to pay. When the conductress turned expectantly toward me, I began to search my pockets in great embarrassment, pretending to look for what I knew was not there at all. As I put my hand into my topcoat pocket, I felt a crisp piece of paper and pulled it out. To my surprise, it was a ten-shilling note. Together, James and I praised the Lord with great delight for this provision.

At Swansea, we changed to a long-distance luxury coach. The remaining money was just enough to pay for one round-trip ticket and one one-way ticket. Since James had to be back at the college the following day, and I was to remain at the church we were visiting for the weekend, he asked me to give him the round-trip ticket and to trust the Lord for my return. I was prepared to do that.

As we sat inside the bus, discussing our predicament, a total stranger knocked on the window from outside, asking us to come out. We both went outside to meet him, and he asked us to join him in another bus in which he was traveling. I could not recall ever having met this gentleman, yet he seemed to know me. He told us he was on his way to the service at which I was supposed to preach.

After the bus was well on its way, I pulled out my guitar, and we began to sing about the Lord. When the conductor came for the fare, I asked for one round-trip ticket for James and one one-way ticket for myself. At this point, without realizing that we were running short of money, the stranger pulled out his wallet and asked the conductor for three round-trip tickets, one for each of us. Once more the Lord had graciously provided for us. As the words of the old Gospel chorus say, "The Lord knows the way through the wilderness; all we have to do is follow."

If I were to recount every miracle the Lord did during my training at the college, it would literally take volumes. No wonder John said in his gospel:

And there are also many other things which Jesus did, the which, if they should be written every one, I suppose that even the world itself could not contain the books that should be written.

But these are written, that ye might believe that Jesus is the Christ, the Son of God; and that believing ye might have life through his name.

John 21:25 and 20:31

I must tell one other incident from this period. It always thrills me to remember it. That coat I reached into and found the ten-shilling note in was a miracle in itself. When I entered the college, all the clothing I had was a single pair of shoes, a single pair of trousers, one jacket and two white shirts (and these had been given to me). I wore those two shirts until the collars were frayed, and I patched them as best I could, until finally they were beyond repair and I could no longer wear them. Although God did many miracles for me, my faith was also tested at times.

During that winter, influenza hit Great Britain, and many were hospitalized. The private hospital of the college was filled to capacity with severe flu cases. Although I did not have any warm clothing, the Lord kept me from colds and any other illness, and I enjoyed perfect health and strength during my stay there.

One evening, just before supper, I received a call from a total stranger, an elderly widower. He told me that while he was praying the Lord had spoken to him and told him to give me one of his coats. He gave me his address and told me to come immediately to his house. When I arrived, he took me to his wardrobe and showed me two coats, wanting me to choose one of them. When I tried on the coat I had chosen, it was exactly my size.

After I had been in the college for a year, my shoes and socks were wearing out. I darned the socks and tried to mend the shoes by sticking cardboard inside the soles. Even though the Lord had done many miracles for me, it had not occurred to me to ask Him for shoes. I did not yet realize that I could ask for *all* my needs and He would supply them. One night I was brought to my knees. I was desperate. It was not easy to walk in snow with worn-out shoes. The cardboard I placed inside the shoes got wet and came apart, and my feet were constantly wet and cold when I went out.

When I was finally driven to talk to God about my clothing needs, I spoke to Him as a son would speak to his father. Knowing that He was the King of kings, and that that made me a prince, I felt that I should be dressed like one. I asked the Lord for a brand-new pair of shoes.

A large convention was being conducted at the college, and among the prominent speakers were Norman Grubb and others who had been involved in the Welsh Revival of 1904. Many missionaries came from all over the world to attend this conference. My duty during their stay was to peel buckets of potatoes for their meals. One day I was bringing some peeled potatoes to the kitchen when someone shouted, "Charles, there's a letter for you on the mail board." I could not imagine who would send me a letter. I had never received mail from anyone at the college, not even from my parents.

When I reached the mail board, I found that the letter was addressed: "To an Indian Student, Bible College of Wales, Swansea." Since I was the only Indian student there at the time, I took the envelope and opened it. There was no letter inside, only a five-pound note, just enough to buy a good pair of shoes and a pair of socks.

I was so excited that God had heard my cry the night before. When I had time to think about it, I realized that the Lord had actually answered my prayer before I had prayed it. The money had been mailed a day before I prayed.

How faithful the Lord is! This confirmed His promise:

Before they call, I will answer; and while they are yet speaking, I will hear. Isaiah 65:24

In my excitement, I told this miracle to everyone I met that day. Then, during a break, I went to downtown Swansea in search of a pair of shoes and some socks. I purchased a pair of black shoes and was looking for a pair of the French-made stretch socks that were popular in England at the time, but time ran out before I could find what I was looking for.

Later, at the college, one of my friends, Jimmy Vananigan, saw my brand new pair of shoes and made a joking remark about them during lunch. That remark reached the ears of Dr. Simmons, and immediately after lunch, he went upstairs to check and see if I had paid my fees for the term. Finding that I still owed something on the account, he sent for me.

As I walked into Dr. Simmons' office, I knew that he would not be very pleased with me. "How did you get those shoes, Charles?" he asked, frowning.

"I prayed, and the Lord sent me money for them," I replied.

"Have you cleared your fees for this term?" he demanded.

"Well, no, I guess I haven't," I admitted with embarrassment.

"Charles, how did you dare to spend this money on yourself, when you knew you still owed money to the college?"

I tried to explain: "I needed shoes very badly. Mine were full of holes, and my feet were always wet and cold. When I prayed for shoes and received some money, I thought the Lord was answering my prayer and giving me shoes."

"Charles, that is not right!" he said. "You should never spend money on yourself when you owe the college. The college should be first, ahead of shoes and other material things. Do you have any money left?"

"Yeeesss," I said hesitantly.

"Hand it over," he said.

When he had counted it, he said, "This will help a bit toward your remaining tuition, but don't ever forget, from now on, that your debt to the college is always first."

I nodded miserably, unable to speak. The money for my new socks had just been taken from me.

The following day all the visiting missionaries and

speakers left. Some of the missionaries had occupied our student rooms, and we had stayed temporarily in lecture rooms. When I returned to my room, I found that my bed had been beautifully made with clean sheets and pillowcases. I picked up my pillow, and to my amazement, I found under the pillow a brand new pair of French-made stretch socks. They were charcoal gray, just the color I had wanted.

In great excitement, I took the socks to Dr. Simmons and shared with him the entire story of how I had wished to buy a pair of black shoes and a pair of charcoal-gray socks to match. Since he had taken the remainder of my money, I had been left without a penny, but the Lord knew the need and met it. We rejoiced together at the providence of God.

I am thankful to God for all my experiences during my training period. He never failed me, and I had come this far by faith, having learned to lean on the Lord, trusting in His Holy Word. He had promised:

But my God shall supply all your need according to his riches in glory by Christ Jesus.

Philippians 4:19

Now I knew that God would never fail me!

1. "Lord, Make Me a Channel of Blessing," author unknown.
2. If the reader would wish to know more about the life and work of Rees Howells, I recommend the book *Intercessor* by Norman Grubb, Christian Literature Crusade, 1987.
3. *Jehovah Jireh (Jehovah the provider)... .*   Genesis 22:14

CHAPTER 3

WITH THE "TEDDY" GANGS IN BIRMINGHAM

I am debtor both to the Greeks, and to the Barbarians;
both to the wise, and to the unwise.   Romans 1:14

The years of rich training in the life of faith which I received at the Bible College of Wales inspired me to launch out into my own ministry, believing God to provide for me. My first mission field was in Birmingham, England, where I found myself ministering to "Teddy" gangs.

The "Teddy" gangs were the toughest groups of youth in England during the fifties and sixties. They were very violent, and vandalism was a serious problem in the neighborhoods they frequented. Churches in some sections of Birmingham were afraid to keep their doors open because of the gang activities. The general public was afraid to walk in the streets after dark, particularly in an area called Balsell Heath, and that is where I chose to begin my ministry.

The young people who made up the gangs were between twelve and seventeen years old. Even at that young age, they committed many serious crimes. Two murders had recently been committed in one of the local parks, and many gangs were known to roam there.

As I began to move among these youths, I felt a great compassion for their souls. With all their outward toughness, I could see the loneliness in their hearts. Filled with compassion, I started to minister the love of Jesus to them.

Guitar music was very popular at the time, so I would take my guitar to their meeting places and sing. Many of these young people gathered at a restaurant owned by a Spaniard. I befriended him, and he permitted me to sing in the restaurant. I sang popular spirituals, such as "Just a Closer Walk With Thee," "He's Got the Whole World in His Hands," and others. I also sang some popular Gospel songs being sung at that time by Elvis Presley and Pat Boone. The singing attracted the young people, and then I would witness to them and give them the Gospel of Jesus Christ. Although none of them made a move right then to accept Christ as their Savior, their interest was clearly aroused to hear more. I did the same at other restaurants, with a similar response.

I decided that I needed to get them away from the public place if they were to respond to the Gospel, so I rented a hall and announced regular Gospel meetings. To my surprise, the place was often filled with young people I had met in the restaurants. One after another, these young toughs were softened by the Gospel and they gave their hearts to Jesus.

Others came to the meetings with something else in mind. They were intent on disturbing the services. They broke out light bulbs and windows. During the preaching, they would make funny remarks loudly enough for everyone to hear, and then they would laugh uproariously. Although I was glad for the souls being saved, my patience was severely tested during this time.

One night, when their disturbance reached the point I could barely stand, I said to myself, *I would like to wring their necks.* Just then the Holy Spirit spoke to me these words, "I have sent you to save their necks, not to wring them." Still, I battled this negative feeling during the rest of that meeting. I later came to realize that my lack of power was due to the fact that I had not received the infilling of the Holy Spirit.

In 1955, I was invited to a service at an Assemblies of God church, the Hockley Pentecostal Mission. A full-Gospel evangelist was holding a series of meetings there. The church itself was pastored by two elderly ladies, Miss Fisher and Miss Reeves, very saintly women.

Although I had briefly attended a Pentecostal church, I had never seen anything like this. It was all new and strange to me, so I sat at the back of the sanctuary with a critical spirit. I found fault with all the preacher's mannerisms and had no place in my heart to understand that the Holy Spirit was at work in him. He seemed oblivious to my bad spirit and went on delivering his message.

At the close of the message, when he gave an altar call for salvation, hundreds of people began streaming forward to be saved. The Holy Spirit began to stir within me and gave me a deep desire to go with them to the altar. Without understanding why I was going, I responded.

Halfway down the aisle I began to reason within myself that it was foolish and unnecessary for me to go to the altar when I was already saved and was, in fact, the pastor of a church. At that moment, the Holy Spirit spoke to my heart and showed me that my attitude made me worse than a sinner. As a Christian, I should have known better than to criticize the ways of the Holy Spirit. The Lord was calling me to true repentance concerning my critical nature. I went on forward to the altar, not knowing what would happen to me there.

As I stood there with the crowd, the evangelist came directly to me. "What do you want, Charles?" he asked.

When he said that, the fear of God fell upon me. We were total strangers, and he had no way of knowing my name. This was the power of God, and I needed it. Without hesitating, I said, "I need the infilling of the Holy Spirit."

He advised me to go to a back room where men of God were praying for those who needed the baptism of the Holy Spirit. As I walked into that room, two men came toward me and asked, "Do you want the baptism of the Holy Spirit, brother?" With a great hunger in my heart, I replied that I did.

One of the brothers raised his hand to touch my brow, but when he was still some two feet away, the Holy Spirit fell on all three of us with such force that each of us fell flat on the floor. As I lay on my back on the floor, I was so filled with God's power that I began to speak in an unknown language. I was absolutely saturated with the Spirit of God.

For several hours I remained on the floor in that condition. When someone finally lifted me from the floor, they asked me to go back inside to give a testimony, and when I tried to comply, I staggered like a drunken man. I was indeed drunk in the Spirit of the living God.

When I stepped onto the platform, Miss Reeves and

Miss Fisher asked me to testify, but I could not speak any other language but the language of the Holy Spirit. Nobody understood what I said that night, but they knew that I was under the influence of God's Spirit. This mighty, unforgettable experience launched me into a much deeper phase of ministry.

From that moment on, I no longer ministered in my own strength. Now I knew what it meant to minister through the Holy Spirit. He took over, and I quickly learned that all I had to do was relax, let go and let God have His way in whatever I was doing.

The very next day, all I wanted to do was to go out and win souls for the Kingdom of God. As Jesus said:

> *Ye shall receive power, after that the Holy Ghost is come upon you: and ye shall be witnesses unto me both in Jerusalem, and in all Judaea, and in Samaria, and unto the uttermost part of the earth.*   Acts 1:8

God's power was what I had been lacking, and I could now offer the power of His love to the "Teddy" boys and girls. I went to their favorite park and stood there singing, "I'm redeemed by the Blood of the Lamb." Just then, thirteen "Teddy" boys, all over six feet tall, started walking toward me. I could tell that they wished to harm me in some way, but as they approached, a love I had never experienced before began welling up in my heart for them. Rivers of love flowed out of me toward those young men.

When they were only twenty feet away from me, a strange thing happened. It was as if their feet became cemented to the ground. They could not move forward any more. The rivers of love seemed to prevent them from approaching me. The Holy Spirit had intervened, and His mighty power had guarded me from harm.

I began to preach, and when I gave an altar call, I saw tears in the eyes of the young people. I knew that something wonderful had happened to them. I asked, "Would you like to receive the love of God in your hearts?" One after the other, they nodded their assent.

"Where would you like to do it?" I asked.

"Right here," they replied.

All thirteen of them fell to their knees right there in the park and gave their hearts to Jesus. This confirmed the Bible promise of Acts 1:8. It took the power of the Holy Spirit to do the work in those hard-hearted youths. God had said:

> *Not by might, nor by power, but by my Spirit, saith the* LORD *of hosts.*   Zechariah 4:6

From then on, I had a wonderful time preaching in that area, and many "Teddy" boys and girls came to Jesus. Those who were saved began to join me in traveling around, preaching and singing. Sometimes we would go into Gloucestershire, Worcestershire and Wellington, hiring a large bus in which to travel. Words are inadequate to describe the glorious things God did among those "Teddy" gangs by His power. I will never forget it and never stop thanking God for it.

CHAPTER 4

MY FIRST MISSIONARY JOURNEY

And Jesus came and spake unto them, saying, All
power is given unto me in heaven and in earth. Go ye
therefore, and teach all nations, baptizing them in the
name of the Father, and of the Son, and of the Holy
Ghost: teaching them to observe all things whatso-
ever I have commanded you: and, lo, I am with you
alway, even unto the end of the world. Amen.

Matthew 28:18-20

After six years of ministering among the "Teddy"
gangs in Birmingham, God gave me a vision for the
world. One weekend I was invited to a church outside
Birmingham to preach. On Saturday, while we were having a prayer meeting at the pastor's house, I saw a vision
of a large globe of the world circling above my head.
Gradually, it drew closer and closer, and I began to pray
within my heart, asking God to explain what this meant.

There were thirty or thirty-five people at the prayer
meeting, and we were all standing in a big circle as we
prayed. My eyes were closed, and I was meditating on
the Lord, when suddenly that big globe came and rested

on my shoulders. I wondered what it meant, and I prayed earnestly for God to make His meaning clear to me — either through the people or directly to me. I had never before had a vision, and I wanted to be sure my experience was scriptural.

While I was meditating on this in my spirit, the entire group gathered around me, and a Scottish evangelist laid his hands on me and began to minister. The power of the Lord was so strong that I fell to the ground. As I lay there, the evangelist had a vision of my future ministry, and he prophesied over me.

In the vision, he saw me preaching Jesus and Him crucified in the midst of a great crowd of dark people. The masses of people present had their hands raised up toward Heaven, praising the Lord for their salvation. He was unable to say which country this might be.

The next day, after I finished my preaching engagement at this church, I returned to Birmingham and immediately began to seek the face of God in thirty days of prayer and fasting. I was still ministering on Sundays among the "Teddy" boys and girls, but I sensed that my life and ministry was changing. The purpose of my fast was to draw closer to God so that I could be led by His Spirit.

On the thirtieth day of my fast, I heard an audible voice speaking to me to go to Kingston, Jamaica. I ate, breaking my fast, and then I started packing for Jamaica.

I knew no one in Kingston who could sponsor me or invite me to a church to preach, but the invitation from the Lord was enough for me. Many scriptures began to come to my mind, such as:

Led by the Master's Hand

As I was with Moses, so I will be with thee: I will not fail thee, nor forsake thee. Be strong and of a good courage. Joshua 1:5-6

The most powerful scriptural passage that encouraged me to take this faith missionary journey was the Great Commission itself. Jesus said He had given me all power and that I should take that power and use it to win men and women all over the world. He promised that I would not go alone. He would go with me *"even unto the end of the world."*

What else did I need? This promise was enough for me to know that I would be well provided for in both spiritual and material necessities. If the Lord Jesus Himself had promised to go with me, what more could I desire? It was encouraging to know that I would not be traveling alone.

The Sunday before I left, I broke the news to the young people at church that I was leaving on a missionary journey. Even though they knew that I was doing the will of God, they were very sad and many wept.

As I was about to preach that day, an elderly English gentleman came into the building and sat toward the back. His eyes were closed throughout much of the service. At first, I felt very uncomfortable with his presence. He was the only older person there, and he apparently was not paying any attention to my preaching at all.

After I finished, I felt led to call the gentleman to the altar. To my surprise, he came forward in a great hurry. I asked him to sit down in the front pew and take his shoe off. I did not realize that the Holy Spirit was moving in His gifts. The man removed one of his shoes, and with my eyes closed, I laid my hands on his heel and prayed for God's healing power to come upon it.

I was not quite sure what I was doing, since I had never moved in the gifts of the Spirit before. During my fasting period, I had felt a deep desire for the spiritual gifts described in the Scriptures. Now, I believed, God had granted the desire of my heart and He was manifesting His power through me in a new way.

For those who wonder if it is scriptural to desire spiritual gifts, it is worthwhile to note what the Apostle Paul had to say on the subject:

> *But covet earnestly the best gifts.*
> 1 Corinthians 12:31

> *Follow after charity [love], and desire spiritual gifts.*
> 1 Corinthians 14:1

As it turned out, this man's heel had been infected and covered with a very serious ulcer, and it had caused him great suffering. He had been scheduled for surgery the next day. Through someone's recommendation, he had come to our service for prayer. That night, after hands were laid on him for his healing, he received a miracle and cried out to God with thanksgiving. He said that when I placed my hands on his heel, he felt a warm feeling run through his leg. He jumped on that heel several times, and miraculously, he felt no pain. The surgery to remove the ulcer was cancelled, and the Lord was glorified.

While I was praying for this man, something happened that I will never forget. I felt two large hands on my shoulders, hands like those of a man who was serving as my assistant pastor. He often stood behind me in support as I prayed for the sick. When I finished praying, I turned around to say to him, "Isn't the Lord wonderful?" To my surprise, there was no one behind me, and my co-pastor was sitting in the congregation. I knew immediately that the hands I had felt had been the invisible, mighty hands of the Lord confirming His sign-gift ministry.

In a back room after the service, the English gentleman who had just been healed of the ulcer came to share his testimony with me. He said he was amazed that on two occasions God used someone from a foreign country to bless him. I knew that he was referring to me since I had prayed for his healing, but I was curious about the other person and in what way he had been a blessing. He proceeded to tell me he was saved under the ministry of a man from Kingston, Jamaica, a man by the name of Pastor Brown. I began to rejoice, knowing that the Lord had sent this man to me for a twofold reason. God was confirming the sign-gift ministry He had given me through the healing of this man, but He was also repeating to me His call for me to go to Kingston, Jamaica. The very next day, I booked my passage on the SS *Coronia* and thus made my way to Jamaica. It was a nineteen-day journey.

Many college students from Spain and a few families going back to Spain and Venezuela were on board. From the very start of the voyage, I had many opportunities to witness to them. Once, I was on the deck playing my guitar and singing Gospel songs, when some of the passengers started gathering around me to hear the music.

Most of them could not understand English, but they were drawn by the music. A few days went by, and almost the entire ship heard about my singing and playing on deck. During this time, the American singer and actor Harry Belafonte was very famous for his interpretation of West Indian folk songs. He sang many calypso songs and hymns with his guitar. My singing and playing reminded these young people of him, and they began to call me "Indian Harry Belafonte."

I found it easy to get the passengers' attention to my testimony and the preaching of the Gospel, but since most of them could not understand English, they needed an interpreter. A Roman Catholic priest was on board, and he was asked to be my interpreter. It was a blessing to have him as my interpreter because, to my surprise, he became very interested in knowing more about my ministry.

Several of the passengers, including some college students, came to me later saying that they were hungry for the truth they had heard. Even though I had not given an open invitation for salvation, they assured me that they had received the Lord Jesus Christ as their personal Savior and Lord during the trip.

I was thrilled to hear them testify. I gave praise to the Lord and advised them to read the Word and pray to the Father in Jesus' name. Our time together seemed very short, and when we parted, I was sad to see them go. I knew, however, that the Lord's hand was on them in a new way.

On the nineteenth day of my voyage, I arrived at Kingston and discovered that I had only two shillings left (approximately thirty cents US). One could not go very far with two shillings in a tourist country like Jamaica. It was not enough to secure lodging or food or even to hire a porter to carry my luggage away from the port, so I unloaded my baggage on the dock and began to pray.

My training served me well. I knew that He who multiplied two fishes and five barley loaves and fed five thousand men besides women and children was well able to provide my needs. I was trusting Him to help me enter Jamaica and evangelize.

While I was walking up and down the dock, I felt the presence of God more strongly than ever before. I was reminded of His promise in the Great Commission:

> *Lo, I am with you alway, even unto the end of the world.*   Matthew 28:20

As I meditated on the Lord, I heard a still small voice within me whispering the name "Jennis." Going over to the crowd of people waiting outside the gates of the wharf, I motioned to the nearest man.

"Would you please call out the name, 'Jennis' to these people?" I asked.

"Are you looking for someone?" returned the young man.

"Yes, I am," I said.

"Might his full name be Jonathan Jennis?" he inquired.

"Yes," I responded in wonder. "Yes, it is."

"Is this man Jonathan Jennis that you are looking for a preacher?" persisted the young man.

I had no idea that there was such a person as Jonathan Jennis in all the world, much less whether or not he was a preacher, but God had given me the name to ask for, so I replied, "Yes, he is," not really knowing in the natural.

With much excitement the young man said, "Bless God, brother, I am he! You must be Charles Doss from England. We have two carloads of people waiting outside to meet you!" Some friends of his in England had told him of my coming, and soon some strong Jamaican men were carrying my luggage to the cars. I was overwhelmed with the goodness of God!

I evangelized in Jamaica every single day from May 1961 to May 1962, with only one day of rest. Crusades were held in auditoriums, tents, prisons, colleges, universities and even in a courthouse. In the town of Palmouth, a judge from the Supreme Court opened his courthouse for me to preach there for a few evenings. Tremendous miracles of healing took place in this courthouse, and many souls were gloriously saved.

During these meetings, people involved in voodoo marched around the building putting curses on us. Instead, we experienced the wonderful outpouring of God's mercy and grace upon the people in the services.

My time in Jamaica was not without trials. When I first arrived in Kingston, the people apparently thought that because I was well dressed I must be rich. Like most of us, they judged by the outward appearance. The New Testament Church of God put me up in a nice apartment they owned, but that was as far as it went. They mistakenly thought I would be able to take care of my personal expenses.

The apartment was well furnished with appliances, but the refrigerator was empty except for a jug of water.

The first couple of days I was able to manage with my small amount of money, but after that, I was forced to do without meals. As surprising as it seems, no one bothered to ask if I had anything to eat.

I was holding two weeks of meetings there in the city of Kingston, and I was getting hungrier as the days went by. This was not fasting; this was starving.

Because of my training in the Bible college, I was not about to let anyone know of my needs. Jesus had said:

But thou, when thou prayest, enter into thy closet, and when thou hast shut thy door, pray to thy Father which is in secret; and thy Father which seeth in secret shall reward thee openly.　　　Matthew 6:6

God had proved Himself faithful to me in England, and He would do so in Jamaica as well. I was sure of it. The name "Jehovah Jireh" had been proudly proclaimed to be faithful in our college, and I knew that God would never deny His faithfulness.

In front of the apartment where I was staying there was a huge mango tree, and it bore an abundance of fruit. Those mangos were big, bigger than a large grapefruit. When I could stand my forced fasting no longer, every morning after prayer I would go out and pick ripe mangos to eat. I had mangos for breakfast, lunch and dinner. I ate mangos for two weeks, until my eyes and my complexion turned yellowish, like the mango.

One night the pastor of the church where I was conducting the special meetings looked at me as we shook hands. "Are you feeling well?" he asked.

"Why, do I look like a mango?" I said, without thinking.

He was speechless when he knew how I had been existing. The next day he came to my apartment. Opening the refrigerator and seeing only mangos spilling out, he broke into tears. He quickly spread the word among his church members, and from that day forth, I was loaded with all kinds of food. Some of the people even brought live pigs and chickens for me to kill and eat. Their gifts were so abundant that I had to graciously turn down the pigs. I couldn't eat it all. What an experience!

The meetings in Kingston were powerful. The Holy Spirit moved in a mighty way, and even the wildest Rastafarians, who came to disturb the meeting, were gloriously saved.

During several weeks, I was introduced to some of the primitive areas of Jamaica, where hundreds of sick and afflicted were miraculously healed due to their childlike faith in the preaching of the Word. In that area, I had to stay in small sheds made of tin. My bed was as hard as a rock, made of wood, but with no mattress. I had to use some of my clothing as a pillow.

No proper water supply was available due to the scarcity of water in those areas. A rusty drum was filled with drinking water, and I felt I had to drink from it without asking any questions. One day, while I was having a drink of that water, however, I saw many small maggots in my glass. I immediately threw away the glass, together with the contaminated water. After that, whenever I became thirsty, I went to a neighbor's hut and drank some black coffee to quench my thirst.

One day, while having a cup of strong, hot coffee, I

felt something brush my lips as I drank from the cup. I thought it might be part of the sugar cane husk left in the sugar. When I had drunk the last of the coffee, I looked inside the cup, only to find a dead scorpion lying inside. Scorpions are highly poisonous, and I was told that if a scorpion dies in any food, it passes its poison on to the food. The person who eats that food can become seriously ill. To my amazement, I did not feel any ill effects from that deadly drink. It was an accident, I am convinced, and not done deliberately. Had I known there was a dead scorpion in the cup, I surely would not have drunk the coffee, no matter how many times I had prayed over it. I knew better than to tempt the Lord.

I could fill a book with the many incidences that often cause missionaries to wonder if they are really called or not. A true missionary, however, is ready to pay any price. When we read the life of the Apostle Paul, we realize that a warrior who is willing to lay down his life for the cause of the Gospel must pass through many fiery trials and tests in order to achieve his goal. Paul wrote:

> *Are they ministers of Christ? (I speak as a fool) I am more; in labours more abundant, in stripes above measure, in prisons more frequent, in deaths oft. Of the Jews five times received I forty stripes save one. Thrice was I beaten with rods, once was I stoned, thrice I suffered shipwreck, a night and a day I have been in the deep; in journeyings often, in perils of waters, in perils of robbers, in perils of mine own countrymen, in perils by the heathen, in perils in the city, in perils in the wilderness, in perils in the sea, in perils among false brethren; in weariness and painfulness, in*

watchings often, in hunger and thirst, in fastings often, in cold and nakedness.

2 Corinthians 11:23-27

During the early sixties, the Rastafarians were creating many problems in Jamaica. There were two sects within their ranks. One group believed that their god was living in Africa and that they were his sons. The other group believed that they were gods themselves.

The Rastafarians lived in the forests and public parks and wandered around in torn clothes, patting their hair with mud and making themselves absolutely ugly. The men grew their beards as long as possible, for the man with the longest beard was thought to be the most spiritual. Their belief was that they should not look handsome or pretty, and to prove their point, they quoted a scripture similar to one in Isaiah 53:2:

There is no beauty that we should desire him.

Isaiah 53:2

These Rastafarians condemned those who dressed neatly and had well-groomed hair, by shouting "Vanity of vanities!" and trying to call down fire from Heaven to burn them. They were setting fire to churches, burning them down, attacking Christians and disturbing Christian meetings. God, however, gave me much favor with them. Not all of them were favorable toward me, but of those who came to my meetings, many were saved.

One unforgettable experience took place in a town where I was staying near a sugarcane field. I was enjoying the quietness. One morning, I was led to go to the sugarcane field to pray. I knelt there about eight in the morning, under the shade of a huge tree at the edge of the field. The Holy Spirit began to pray through me in tongues. When I rose from my knees, it was well after 8:00 P.M. The sun had already gone down, and the moon was risen in the sky. I had been on my knees in the Spirit for more than twelve hours, but I was not hungry, thirsty or even tired. Instead, I felt unusually strong and energized.

I suddenly realized, however, that I was an hour late for the service. The Gospel meeting had already begun, and the pastors were wondering what had happened to me. I rushed to my little cottage, shaved, dressed and hurried to the meeting place. The building was packed to capacity, and a crowd had also gathered outside. It was such a large crowd, in fact, that it was impossible for me to get in through the front door. The only way I could get to the platform was to go behind the church building and climb a wooden ladder that led to a door behind the pulpit.

As I approached the back of the building, I saw, hiding there, a Rastafarian man. I sensed that he had been sent to sever my head for a burnt offering. The Rastafarians, in those days, were known to practice human sacrifice whenever they could. For them to take the life of a Christian missionary and use him for a burnt offering was considered to be the best type of sacrifice.

I saw that he was hiding under the wooden ladder, waiting for me to come around the building. I had no idea how he knew that I would be coming that way. As I looked at his face, I saw his eyes bulging out, staring into mine with an evil look. Immediately, the Holy Spirit revealed to me that he had a long knife hidden behind his back and that he was influenced by a spirit of murder to try to kill me.

I had no fear of him or of death, and I began to talk to him. The Spirit of holy boldness and heavenly wisdom began to flow through me. I first asked him if he was happy, and he replied in a firm voice, "I am happiness," revealing that he was from the group that believed they were gods. The Lord gave me wisdom that I should not talk with him further, but should advise him to come into the building or stand in front of the building to hear the service. I went up the ladder, stepped onto the platform, shut the door behind me and pushed the piano in front of the door. The twelve hours I had spent praying in the Spirit were to prepare me to face this situation. The Lord had made me bold and wise, and I had escaped the chilly hand of death.

As I stepped onto the platform, I immediately announced that there was a man outside with a spirit of murder and that we needed to sing the hymn "There Is Power in the Blood." As the congregation sang the song, through the window I saw the man raise his knife toward the sky and run violently into the thick woods nearby and disappear.

A tremendous service resulted! Many were saved and there were outstanding physical healings. Also, seventy-five people received the baptism in the Holy Spirit with the evidence of speaking in tongues, without hands ever being laid on them.

Some days later, in Clarkstown, I was staying alone in a ramshackle house that was overrun with rats and cockroaches. The ceiling had several holes, and I often saw big rats peek through them. At night, while I was asleep, rats would literally fall onto my bed, and I would be awakened. One night I went into the kitchen to get a glass of water. As soon as I turned on the light, I could hear big cockroaches scurrying for cover. They were all over the walls, the counters and the cupboards. Going after a glass of water in that kitchen was not an inviting prospect.

Through all this, I had an inner peace and joy that I was being *Led by the Master's Hand* in Jamaica, and I was happy to be winning souls for Him.

Early one morning when I got up to go out, I discovered one of my shoes missing. After fruitlessly searching all over, I was forced to wear another pair. Late that evening, a little girl brought me the missing shoe. She had found it in the marketplace. It had some teeth marks in the leather. Evidently one of the big rats, or "bandicoots," as we called them, must have picked up the shoe and carried it away. After nibbling on it a while, it had lost interest and dropped it in the street. What a place to find it!

Many of the men and women of that particular town had lived together without being married and had even raised large families. When they came to the meetings and surrendered their lives to Christ, things began to change. They either separated or were married legally. This caused a stir in the town. Many of the local men were angry with me because they lost their illicit companions.

During one Sunday morning service, I was standing on the platform preaching to a large crowd. The platform and the space before the altar were so filled with men, women and children that I had very little room to move about. Right in the middle of my preaching the Lord gave me a word of knowledge that there was a man standing outside the building who was deeply troubled and angry with me. My heart was moved with compassion, and I wished to see him delivered from his hatred. I spoke it out: "There is a man standing outside the building who needs deliverance from hatred and bitterness."

Suddenly, I heard a young man screaming at the top of his voice. He was saying, "I am the man! I am the man!" He came into the building and rushed toward me through the crowd. Stopping about twenty-five to thirty feet away, he raised his hand and threw a dagger at me. I did not know which way to turn, since I was locked into a small space on the platform by crowd. All I could do was plead the blood of Jesus. I had an open Bible in my hands, and I stood still looking steadily at him.

The dagger came flying toward me, then suddenly, when it was just two or three feet from me, it turned downward and stuck into the wooden floor. Overcome with relief, I knew that God's wall of fire was standing round about me. Looking back now, I rejoice to know that so many wonderful promises in the Bible are ours to claim and live by:

> *When thou passest through the waters, I will be with thee; and through the rivers, they shall not overflow thee: when thou walkest through the fire, thou shalt not be burned; neither shall the flame kindle upon thee.*
> Isaiah 43:2

Led by the Master's Hand

Yea, though I walk through the valley of the shadow of death, I will fear no evil: for thou art with me; thy rod and thy staff they comfort me.   Psalm 23:4

Thou shalt not be afraid for the terror by night; nor for the arrow that flieth by day; nor for the pestilence that walketh in darkness; nor for the destruction that wasteth at noonday. A thousand shall fall at thy side, and ten thousand at thy right hand; but it shall not come nigh thee.   Psalm 91:5-7

Another strange incident took place in that same town. I was preaching in a smaller church when the Holy Spirit showed me another man standing outside the building. The Spirit showed me that he was suffering with asthma and that he was living a very sinful life. I called out to him to come inside the building and get right with God, assuring him that the Lord would forgive him and heal his body. Those who were outside urged him to answer my call, pleading with him to go inside and be healed, but he stubbornly hardened his heart and would not come.

I warned the man a second time that he might not have another day to live and that that night might be his last chance to be saved. Despite these warnings, he turned his back and went home.

The following morning, some children knocked on my door. When I opened it, they took me by the hand to show me what had happened. Apparently, this man had gone to the sugar field early that morning and had suffered a serious asthma attack there. He appeared to have tried to get back to the safety of his shack, but he fell down at the doorstep and died right there.

I had the opportunity to preach to the crowd that was standing around the body. The fear of the Lord fell on the people, and they knelt down right there and gave their hearts to Jesus. I was reminded of the fifth chapter of Acts, especially verse 11:

And great fear came upon all the church, and upon as many as heard these things.   Acts 5:11

As we follow the Holy Spirit's leading, we are continuing the Acts of the Apostles today. It was happening for me in Jamaica.

CHAPTER 5

A MISSIONARY JOURNEY
TO THE USA

*And he went ... and spake boldly for the space of three
months, disputing and persuading the things concerning the kingdom of God.*   Acts 19:8

After I had spent a year evangelizing in Jamaica, the
Lord began to place America on my heart, and I felt the
call to minister in the United States and Canada. I had
no contacts in those countries. My only contact was with
the Lord of the Harvest, and wherever He led me, I
would go.

I was invited to Kingston Garden to dedicate a new
church opened in response to the many converts coming into the Kingdom. In the opening service, I preached
and prayed for the Holy Spirit's special blessings upon
the work and the workers. To my surprise, three Americans were in the congregation that day: an elderly lady,
her son and her daughter-in-law. After hearing me
preach, the lady, Mrs. Rebecca Johnson, felt that I should
be ministering in the United States. She didn't say anything to me at the time, as she was reluctant to approach
a total stranger.

A Missionary Journey to the USA

The next morning, I left Kingston for Montego Bay with the pastor of the Kingston church, who had offered to drive me there. Several miles outside of Kingston, he stopped the car and told me that he felt it was the Lord's will for me to stay with him one more night and leave for Montego the next day. I sensed that he was right, so we turned around and went back to Kingston.

As we approached the pastor's house, we saw Mrs. Johnson standing outside. She had been praying for God to confirm His will to invite me to the United States and had asked the Lord that if it was indeed His will He would bring me back to Kingston. The Lord confirmed this by doing exactly what she had asked. This miracle gave her the courage to extend to me the invitation.

Mrs. Johnson was living in Richmond, Indiana. After receiving her invitation, I prayed for the Lord's guidance and provision for my trip — as had become my custom. One day while I was praying, I had a vision. A green Chevrolet station wagon appeared before me. It was picking me up at the Miami Beach harbor. I was surprised by this because I did not know anyone in the Miami area. I was excited about what God had in store for me, and I began to prepare earnestly for my missionary trip to the United States and Canada.

I applied for an American visa and, to my disappointment, my application was denied. I went into the American consular office in Kingston personally to appeal for a visa, but every time I went, the answer was negative. In my heart I knew that the Lord was leading me, and I wondered why I was being denied. I prayed again and the Lord spoke to my heart and said, "As I was with Moses, so will I be with you." He assured me that I would get the visa and be able to minister in the United States and Canada and that nothing would hinder me.

One day, as I waited again to see the consul, I heard him remarking that everyone in Jamaica wanted to go to the United States, and it seemed that all of them used religion as some sort of excuse. He was sure they were all phonies. He then walked out of the office in a huff, right in front of me — even though he knew I was waiting to see him.

This temporary setback did not diminish my enthusiasm. I determined in faith to complete all my arrangements for the journey. I went to a photo studio and had passport photos taken for my visa, and then I went back to the consulate, fully expecting to receive a visa. This time the vice-consul called me into his office. "Just why do you wish to visit the United States?" he asked.

He was so pleasant and easy to talk to that my courage rose, and I replied, "Sir, when Jesus said to go into all the world and preach the Gospel to every creature, He included America and all Americans as well."

"How long would you like to stay?" the vice-consul asked.

"A month or two would be very much appreciated," I said.

"You will need far more than a month or two to spread the Gospel over such a vast country," he told me. "How about a four-year unlimited-entry visa, to give you enough time to complete your mission?" He asked it with a smile.

A Missionary Journey to the USA

I was dumbfounded. From no entry at all, the Lord had brought me to a man who was willing to allow me four years and multiple entries! Gratefully I replied, "Thank you, sir, and may the Lord bless you!"

Smiling, he approved my application and then directed me to another section for the proper stamp. As I stood there with the long-sought visa in my hand, I was sure that the Lord would provide the rest of my needs for this missionary journey. He has promised:

Faithful is he that calleth you, who also will do it.
1 Thessalonians 5:24

Within a matter of a few days, the money for my passage was miraculously provided, and I was on my way to Miami Beach, Florida.

I had a pleasant four-day cruise from the British West Indies to the United States. During this voyage, I encountered many interesting people from various parts of the States who were returning home from abroad. At first, I was reluctant to associate with any of them, since I had never come in close contact with many Americans before. Also, I had heard reports of racial prejudice existing among some Americans at the time, and this was another reason to be cautious. I didn't know what to expect.

After we had been at sea for several days, I was relaxing on deck one day when two of the passengers approached me and struck up a conversation. They asked me what I did and why I was going to America. This gave me an opportunity to witness to them. Soon, several other passengers joined us, and I had more people to whom I could witness. By the end of that encounter, the first two passengers and several others had given their hearts to Jesus.

Dr. Clyde Sutter was one of the passengers. A heart specialist, he was an atheist. He became convinced of the existence of God and gave his heart to Christ. A lady who was suffering great depression and had even attempted suicide during the trip found relief from all her depression after she gave her heart to Jesus. Interest was stirred in other professionals who were on the ship as well.

I was very impressed with the friendliness of these tourists and regretted my earlier suspicions of their possible racial prejudice towards me. They were very kind to me all through the voyage.

As we approached Miami Beach, the beautiful countryside lured me into thinking how wonderful it would be to take a week's vacation there before continuing my journey. Holding meetings in Jamaica for a full year with only one day's break had been intense. It would be nice to relax for a few days. The problem was that I did not know anyone in Miami Beach, and I didn't have money for a vacation.

As we went through customs and immigration, Dr. Sutter, who knew nothing about my thoughts of wanting to rest in Miami, approached me and said, "Charles, you have been a great inspiration to all of us. I would like you to be my guest in my home for a week or two. You can relax before you go on with your ministry." Oh, how faithful is our God!

As we waited at the Miami harbor for clearance from customs, the doctor asked his nurse, Mrs. Nina VanThoff, to take a taxi home and bring back a station wagon to haul our luggage. It turned out to be the green Chevrolet station wagon I had seen in my vision while praying in Jamaica.

After I had stayed with Dr. Sutter for a few days, I felt that I should move on to Richmond, Indiana. The believers had scheduled me to minister there. Not realizing how far Indiana was from Florida and what it cost to get there, I was planning to travel by train. When Dr. Sutter and I arrived at the railway station for my departure, he handed me an envelope and said, "The stationmaster presents you with a railway ticket." Apparently, he had already purchased a ticket for my journey to Indiana and wanted to surprise me at the station. Our God is full of surprises! It is a thrill to serve such a mighty God!

The pastor of the church where I was scheduled to minister in Richmond, a total stranger to me, was unaware of the nature of my ministry and of the fact that I moved in the life of faith. Not realizing that I did not have sufficient funds to take care of my personal expenses, she provided a small room for me in the church building, but no other provisions. Night after night I preached my heart out in the church. Many souls were gloriously saved, backsliders were restored, the sick were healed, and Christians were set on fire for God. After each service, I was worn out and went to bed on an empty stomach. Since I had no money to eat out and no transportation to get to a restaurant if I had had the money, I just stayed in my room.

As had happened at the first in Jamaica, God was testing my faith in this new land. I would not ask anyone for help. Although I have never doubted the fact that

God uses people to meet our needs, I was not about to extend my hand to the arm of the flesh.

The Apostle Paul wrote:

> *Not that I speak in respect of want: for I have learned, in whatsoever state I am, therewith to be content. I know both how to be abased, and I know how to abound: every where and in all things I am instructed both to be full and to be hungry, both to abound and to suffer need.* Philippians 4:11-12

Finally, after many days of forced fasting, someone from the congregation invited me for dinner. From that day on, there were several dinner invitations. Had these people known that I was in need, they would have been more than happy to care for me. I was happy to show the Lord that I was willing to give my life as a living sacrifice for His service. As we give our lives for Him, God is faithful to give to us *"good measure"* through men and women who obey Him. Jesus said:

> *Give, and it shall be given unto you; good measure, pressed down, and shaken together, and running over, shall men give into your bosom. For with the same measure that ye mete withal it shall be measured to you again.* Luke 6:38

During the time I was ministering in Indiana, I was invited to attend a tent meeting in Cincinnati, Ohio. Evangelist A.A. Allen was holding a week's revival in his big white-top tent. I was very interested in hearing him preach, since I had read his life story, *My Cross.* The book had been a blessing to me while I was in England, and I was always eager to meet great men of God.

I can never forget what happened the Thursday night I attended Brother Allen's tent meeting. The big tent was packed that night. I was seated in the third row directly in front of the platform, anxiously waiting to hear Brother Allen. I had been told that he was bold, daring and feared no man — only God. As soon as he approached the pulpit, he looked straight at me, pointed his finger at me and said, "The man in the suit ... That brown-skinned man ... Yes, you ... Come over here."

I was shocked! I went forward, anxious to hear what he had to say to me. He took hold of my hand and said to the masses of people, "Here is a man sent from God to our nation to declare the Gospel. Signs, wonders and miracles will follow his ministry." Then he handed the microphone to me and said, "Preach it! Tonight is your night!" And then he sat down. Just like that, I was given the opportunity to minister to his crowd.

I was inspired to preach on Elijah and the need for Elisha's double-portion anointing to reach the unreached nations, such as my native India. While I was preaching, Brother Allen sat at the edge of the platform weeping with compassion for souls in India and other unreached nations.

Attending the meeting were many sick, some lying in stretchers, others in wheelchairs, and many of them seriously ill with incurable diseases. At the close of the service, I had the privilege of standing by the man of God as he prayed the prayer of faith for the healing and deliverance of the sick.

After the service, I was about to leave for Dayton,

Ohio, to be with the Voice of Healing evangelists, when Brother Allen sent his organist to bring me to his trailer. He urged me to stay with him one more night. I stayed with Brother and Sister Allen that night in their two-bedroom suite at a local hotel. He put me in the larger of the two rooms, the one with the king-size bed, while the two of them stayed in the smaller room. I did not want them to give up the larger room for me, and I offered to stay in the smaller room, but Brother Allen would not have it any other way. He said to me, "My guest must have the very best." I thought that was very kind of him.

From that day until Brother Allen went to be with the Lord, whenever I attended his crusades, he would have me join him on the platform while he prayed for the sick and the afflicted. It was quite an experience to watch the man pray with such compassion, yet with such authority, and to watch men and women set free from every conceivable type of sickness and debility.

After those glorious services with Brother Allen, I went to Dayton, Ohio, for another tent meeting held by some of the Voice of Healing evangelists. Among them were James Dunn, David Nunn, W.V. Grant, Sr., Morris Cerullo and several others. It was there that I met Dr. Gordon Lindsay, and he shared with me his vision for the Voice of Healing ministries. He invited me to join the organization and be one with many of the leading ministers of the day. My desire was to be *Led by the Master's Hand,* since I had chosen to be His love slave.

I ministered in Richmond, Indiana, for several weeks in various churches. One day a young couple approached me about joining me in the ministry. They were talented musicians and singers and felt that the three of us would make an effective ministry team. I prayed about it and felt that it was, indeed, the will of God that the three of us form a team. Together we traveled from Indiana to Florida, preaching in several churches on the way.

When we arrived in Sarasota, Florida, I was led to call Brother Gerald Derstine, a man who had been highly recommended to me by the pastors of several churches where I had been preaching. This gracious man immediately opened his arms of fellowship to me.

When I met Dr. Derstine personally, he gave me a warm embrace and said, "Brother Doss, you be a blessing to our people, and God will bless you." Those words have stuck with me all these years. Brother Derstine asked me to stay with him and teach the faith of God. We began with one service and continued for over three months. Many Mennonite families were gloriously saved, healed and delivered during these meetings.

After these meetings at the Gospel Crusade in Sarasota, Florida, Brother Derstine and his family planned to take an extensive trip throughout the United States and parts of Canada. The day before he left, he invited me to join them. He wanted me to have the opportunity to minister among the Mennonite and Amish people. I felt it was the Lord's way of opening the door to other parts of the United States and Canada.

I accepted his invitation, and together we ministered among the Full Gospel Business Men and in various conventions of the Amish and Mennonite people. Many other doors began to open for my ministry through this gracious man's favor. Needless to say, there were many souls saved and numerous healings and deliverances in these meetings.

Led by the Master's Hand

Of all the churches I visited in this period, one stands out in my memory. A businessman by the name of Bill Swad, Sr., a prominent automobile dealer in Columbus, Ohio, and the president of the Columbus chapter of the Full Gospel Business Men's Fellowship, heard me speak in one of his chapter meetings and invited me to his church, the Fairmore First Assembly of God. We began with one week's special meetings, and God moved in a mysterious and wonderful way. A mighty outpouring of the Holy Spirit occurred in every service. Signs, wonders and miracles followed the preaching of the Word each and every night.

During that week, many had visions, and the congregation experienced some unusual manifestations from God. One night I was playing my guitar and singing on the platform with my eyes closed. After finishing my solo, I opened my eyes and found almost the whole congregation on the floor. Some were flat on their faces weeping and saying, "I see Jesus!" Others said, "I see the prophets Moses and Elijah!" Some began to relate the apostles' names. This news spread to various parts of Ohio and drew many people to the services, both Christians and non-Christians.

One businessman's wife saw angelic hosts following Jesus through various parts of the town and finally coming into the building where we were holding the services. She saw the entire church filled with angels, with various instruments, playing heavenly music. That week, every unbeliever who came to our services was saved. They came from all those parts of town where that woman had seen Jesus walking.

A spiritual awakening in my own ministry and in the

city of Columbus, Ohio, resulted from these meetings. To this day, people who were in those services (including Brother Swad) classify those meetings as an earthshaking revival.

Seeing Christians confessing their faults to one another and asking each other for forgiveness was a common occurrence in those meetings. As the Scriptures teach:

> *Confess your faults one to another, and pray one for another, that ye may be healed.*   James 5:16

When we see Christians begin to humble themselves and repent, confessing their faults to one another and praying for one another, there will always be a mighty move of the power of God. This is what we were experiencing.

It was such a blessing to minister in the United States and Canada. Things had gone very well for me in America, and my ministry was in such demand that I sensed that God wanted to establish my work right here. Within a very few months, the Lord blessed me with a home and an incorporated ministry in Arizona, with a group of men who served as my board of directors.

Chapter 6

The Macedonian Call to Java, Indonesia

And a vision appeared to Paul in the night; There stood a man of Macedonia, and prayed him, saying, Come over into Macedonia, and help us. And after he had seen the vision, immediately we endeavored to go.

Acts 16:9-10

My friend Gerald Derstine, while on a missionary journey in Indonesia, described my ministry to various churches and encouraged them to invite me to hold crusades in their country.

In September of 1962, while holding a series of meetings among the Mennonites in Nappanee, Indiana, I received a letter of invitation from one of the Presbyterian churches in Java. Someone handed me the letter one evening at dinner, and even before I opened it, I sensed in my spirit the urgency of the message it contained. I excused myself from the table to read the letter privately. As I read, the Holy Spirit stirred within me a deep compassion for the Christians in Indonesia, and I began to weep. The pastor said that many Indonesian believers had been overcome by persecution, and some had even denied their faith in Christ.

For a long while, the burden for Indonesia was heavy on my heart, and now I decided to go there to minister faith to the churches and stir them up for Jesus. I felt so strongly about going to Indonesia that I was led to cancel all the meetings I had scheduled in the United States and Canada.

It wasn't easy to cancel the upcoming meetings. Some of the ministers who were expecting me had done much planning for these special meetings, and they could not easily understand why I suddenly needed to leave for Indonesia. I knew, however, that I had to obey the Lord's command.

My call to Indonesia was similar to the Macedonian call of the Apostle Paul. He was called to go to Macedonia because of the great need in that region. Before he received this call, he had attempted to preach in Phrygia and the region of Galatia, but he was forbidden by the Holy Spirit. In Mysia he attempted to do the same, but the Spirit of the Lord again prevented him. As he was pondering one night what these things could mean, he received a vision of a man of Macedonia beseeching him to come over to his country and help his people. Paul immediately left to go into Macedonia in obedience to that vision.

In the period of the first-century church, the servants of the Lord leaned heavily on the guidance of the Holy Spirit. They did not simply schedule something without first knowing that it was God's will. The writer of the Proverbs admonishes us:

Led by the Master's Hand

Trust in the LORD with all thine heart; and lean not unto thine own understanding. In all thy ways acknowledge him, and he shall direct thy paths.

Proverbs 3:5-6

I left Nappanee, Indiana, and drove to Fort Washington, Pennsylvania, staying several nights at the WEC (Worldwide Evangelization Crusade) headquarters to fellowship with missionary friends there. Some medical missionaries among them offered their services for my required vaccinations, and others encouraged me with their prayers. These missionaries were trained to live by faith, just as I had been taught in Bible college. I had to rely on that training now, for my finances were very low, not even sufficient to buy enough gasoline to get me to San Francisco, California, where I had made reservations on a ship bound for Indonesia.

I began driving west, trusting solely in the Lord's provision. Driving back through the state of Indiana, I noticed that I was running low on gasoline, and no longer had funds to buy any. Still, I had perfect peace, knowing that the Lord would supply all my need *"according to his riches in glory by Christ Jesus."* As I drove, I leaned forward and opened the glove compartment to get some Kleenex. To my surprise, there was an envelope lying on top of the Kleenex box. On the front of it, someone had written, "Dear Charles, may your song 'He Is My Everything' be a reality to you during this faith missionary journey." I opened the envelope, and there I found a substantial sum of money. Tears sprang to my eyes, as I was reminded that Jesus is, indeed, my Everything.

The Macedonian Call to Java, Indonesia

From earth to glory, He is all I need,
My breath, my sunshine, my friend indeed,
My joy, my peace, my life, eternity through,
He is my everything. Now, how about you?

Just before leaving Pennsylvania, I had called the Indonesian Consulate in San Francisco, to inquire about a visa for Indonesia and was told that it would take at least three months to secure one. I found that impossible to accept. I was determined to get to Java within two months, and the journey by sea would take about six weeks. Plans were already being made for the crusade to start in Jakarta, the capital city. Although I had been told it would be impossible to obtain the visa in such a short time, I knew that with God nothing was impossible. Since my journey was a faith venture, I had determined to go ahead and sail to Java, trusting the Lord to provide the necessary documents for my entry into the country.

By the time I reached San Francisco, the Lord had met all of my financial needs for the voyage. I purchased my ticket and got on board the ship, trusting God for the visa. The purser hurriedly collected our passports and showed us to our cabins. For some reason, none of the passports were examined for the proper documentation, so no one noticed that I had no visa. Later, I learned that the ship had been behind schedule and that this was the reason the crew had been hurried. It proved to be a blessing for me.

The following day, when we were far out to sea, the passports were checked, and the purser discovered his mistake. He came to my cabin with a worried look to question me about why I had no visa for Indonesia. Nothing I said could satisfy him. Just before I left San Francisco, I had informed the Indonesian Consulate that I was leaving for Indonesia — with or without my visa, and it had been without.

Legally, I was not allowed to land in Jakarta without a visa, so I was informed, but as a British citizen, I could enter any British colony without a visa. I would have no problem entering Bangkok or Singapore, where the ship would make stops before reaching Indonesia. I still had time to believe God for the miracle, and I sensed that it was already done.

It was a stormy time of year in the Pacific. During the months of September and October, Southeast Asia often experiences strong monsoons and typhoons, and they are especially powerful in the open sea. Our small cargo ship, with its few passenger cabins, was not in the best of condition. We learned that it had been scheduled for demolition two years earlier, but had been spared and kept in service. Now it was caught in the middle of one of the Pacific storms.

The radio officer received a message that a one-hundred-sixty-mile-an-hour wind was heading in our direction. As we headed into the storm, in fact, some of the instruments on deck were destroyed by the boisterous wind and waves. Things got so bad that all of us (nine passengers) were told to stay in our cabins with our portholes and doors locked tightly. We were not to go on deck. It was covered with water, and the ship was dipping wildly into the sea. To feel the ship roll and pitch with the waves was a frightening experience.

After we were tossed around like a cork for a while,

the captain of the ship was nearly out of his mind with worry, and most of the passengers and even some of the crew members were seasick and frightened. In the middle of all this, the Lord gave me perfect peace. I was sitting on my bed when I heard a still small voice saying, "I am in the hinderpart of the ship, as I was with Peter, and My presence is with you. I have not changed." This gave me great courage, and stirred my faith.

The Holy Spirit spoke to me and said that I could speak the same words that Jesus had spoken to the wind and waves (see Mark 4:39). I could do it in His name, and the wind and waves would obey Him and become calm. I left my cabin, opened the door to the deck, and was amazed to find it completely covered with water. I felt compelled to walk through the water and speak to the troubled ocean in the name of Jesus.

As I struggled through the water, I could see electric eels and other sea creatures swimming in it, as they would in the open ocean. It was a miracle in itself for me to get to the rails without being stung by one of those deadly eels. I managed to grasp the rail at the edge of the deck, and when I did, I took a deep breath and then spoke with authority, commanding the wind and waves to be still in Jesus' name. Satisfied that I had obeyed the Spirit, I returned to my cabin and went to sleep.

About five the next morning I awoke to find the ship sailing smoothly as we approached Manila. I was later told by a naval radio officer that even after the wind of such a storm ceases, it takes a few days for the ocean to settle and become calm again. When Jesus commanded the wind and waves to be still, there was a spontaneous response. The Bible says:

Led by the Master's Hand

And the wind ceased, and there was a great calm.
Mark 4:39

Even though the response had not been immediate when I spoke to the storm in His name, our deliverance was just as miraculous, for, within hours, the ocean became calm.

That morning the passengers were having breakfast with the captain and were discussing the mysterious calming of the ocean. Later, the captain told me he had come to the conclusion that I might have some magic power. He had watched me from the ship's bridge as I had walked across the deck to the railing. At first, he imagined that I was trying to commit suicide. When he realized I was not attempting to jump and heard me shouting, he thought I must be losing my mind. I took the opportunity to witness to him about the power of God, telling of my command to the ocean in Jesus' name. To my surprise, he sat down to hear everything I had to say.

After a long conversation about the unfailing Word of God and the power in the name of Jesus, the captain began to yield to the Spirit of God. I urged him to give his heart to Jesus in true repentance and be filled with His Holy Spirit. At the conclusion of our conversation, he addressed me as "Brother Doss," instead of Mr. Doss, and thus showed me respect. He assured me that he would seek the Lord. He also asked for any literature I could share with him concerning my Christian walk with God.

Another witness to the power of God's providence was a message the purser received from shore that very day. When he came to my door, he said to me, "This time I have good news for you."

Before he could declare it, I said to him, "It's my visa, isn't it?"

He was surprised that I knew and joyfully declared, "Yes!"

He told me that the consul general in San Francisco had wired my visa authorization to both Bangkok and Singapore to make sure that I received it before I reached Indonesia. Jesus never fails!

Upon my arrival in Jakarta, the believers there gave me a warm reception and assured me that there would be a good response in our crusades. Many Indonesian Christians were fasting and praying for a great outpouring of the Holy Spirit. They felt that the time had come for the fulfillment of the many prophecies that had come forth in congregations throughout their nation in recent years.

When the meetings began in Jakarta, the auditorium was filled to capacity, and many people were standing outside the building anxiously waiting to hear the Word of God. After praise and worship, a respected Indonesian Christian leader, Brother John DeFraites, introduced me to the audience. I was thrilled to see such a large crowd of people in the first meeting and began to praise God out loud. During my praising, my words began to change from English into an unknown tongue. I saw the entire congregation stand up with their hands raised toward Heaven, glorifying God while I was praising in the Spirit. I turned around and asked Brother John what they were saying.

"Didn't you know what you were saying?" he asked me with unconcealed excitement.

"No, I didn't," I told him.

"But you were speaking fluent Indonesian," he exclaimed, "and you said, 'Let us stand up and give God the glory!' That's why all the people stood up and praised. I thought you knew how to speak Indonesian!"

"I've never spoken Indonesian before in my life, that I know," I said. At that moment I knew that the Holy Spirit was empowering my ministry in that place. It was the beginning of great things in Indonesia, and I knew, without a shadow of a doubt, that God's Spirit was about to do wonders in that place for His glory.

Sure enough, night after night the Lord confirmed His Word with signs and wonders. Many souls were gloriously saved, and there were miraculous healings in every service. Meetings continued late into the night and sometimes lasted until the following day. The hunger in the hearts of those precious people grew deeper daily. The good news of God's miracle-working power quickly spread throughout the island and even into the neighboring islands. Other doors were soon opened for this ministry of love and compassion to spread beyond the capital.

Bishop Tan Ik Tjiang of Garedja Isa Almase, the Church of the Lord Jesus Christ, was my interpreter in one of the largest churches in Semarang, a large city in central Java. Bishop Tan had a great burden for the churches all over Indonesia and had prayed for years for God to send a man after His own heart with the faith message. The most remarkable thing that took place in Semarang was that small children and young people were so stirred that many of them are in the ministry today because of the visitation of God's Holy Spirit on their lives during those meetings in 1962.

One night the local polio hospital sent several crippled children to the meeting for prayer. I was preaching a faith-stirring message entitled "Slaying the Giant." Halfway through the message the crippled children began removing their braces from their legs, throwing them down and stepping on them, as David had stepped on Goliath to slay him. These children had not been prayed for yet, nor had anyone laid hands on them. The power of God moved on them, and they were instantly healed.

A little four-year-old girl tried to walk but could not. She fell on her face and cried bitterly. Her father consoled her, although he had tears in his own eyes. My heart went out to her, and the Holy Spirit spoke to me a message for her. I told her father not to worry about the present situation because his daughter would grow up straight, strong and healthy, to the glory of God.

When I returned to Indonesia twenty-one years later, I was preaching in a town called Ungaran. An older gentleman brought a young lady, tall and erect, and presented her to me saying, "This is the fulfillment of the prophecy that the Lord gave us through you in 1962." There stood the proof. I was blessed to see the faithfulness of God in fulfilling His promise in this girl's life. She was now twenty-five and a picture of perfect health. May all the glory be unto our God!

During my meetings of 1962, another prophecy came forth upon a young man by the name of Samuel Elkana. I was staying in his parents' home, and one day his father asked me to pray that Samuel would be restored from his backslidden condition. Samuel had gotten very worldly, and his new lifestyle had broken his parents' hearts. I spoke to the young man and told him the Lord was going to restore him and use him mightily in Indonesia. He did not believe the prophecy then.

In 1983, I received an invitation to return to Indonesia, and the invitation came from Samuel himself. Just as the Lord had said in the prophecy in 1962, He had indeed restored Samuel and filled him with the Holy Spirit. Samuel now had a great apostolic ministry in Central Java. He was, in fact, the pastor in Ungaran, and it was while I was ministering in his place, known as Prayer Mountain, that the girl whose healing had been prophesied in 1962 gave her testimony. Praise God! His Word will never return unto Him void (see Isaiah 55:11).

During that first Indonesian missionary journey, I was given the privilege of speaking for five days at a very large Presbyterian church in Malang. The night before the crusade began, the pastor of the church asked me to greet the people. As a way of introduction, he asked me to sing my song "He Is My Everything." Apparently the church was not accustomed to singing accompanied by a guitar, for as I sang, some of the people laughed, and some were obviously uncomfortable. A little disappointed, I abruptly ended my song and prepared to leave the building. Just before I did that, however, I reminded the people that the crusade would be starting the next day and assured them, "God is going to move by His Spirit."

As I was leaving, the pastor came running after me to be sure I was not offended by the way the people had acted. "No," I assured him, "although I was a little disappointed in their attitude."

The following day as we were being driven to the meeting, we ran into a traffic jam about two miles from the church. Vehicles were moving so slowly that it took us a considerable time to reach our destination. To our amazement, we found that the crowd was all heading toward our meeting. The church was jam-packed, and there was hardly any standing room left. The words I had spoken the previous night, "God is going to move by His Spirit," had been taken very seriously by the people, and the news had spread throughout the town.

Two years prior to my visit, an elderly Chinese lady had stood up in the Presbyterian church service and prophesied that God was going to move by His Spirit in that church. Just as abruptly as she had spoken, she sat down. Ever since then, the church had prayed every morning for the fulfillment of that prophecy. Even the children, before they went to school, would go to church at seven in the morning to pray for the moving of the Spirit. The talk of the town was that the prophecy which had been spoken two years before was about to be fulfilled in these meetings. The whole town was stirred. While it is true that some had come to the meetings out of curiosity, many others had come with great expectation.

That first evening, the Lord gave me a short message of love and told me to tell the people that all they needed to do was to thank Him for His finished work at Calvary. I called the people to raise their hands and thank the Lord Jesus for salvation. There was no room to give an altar call, since the building was packed, and every possible space was taken. The people raised their hands in one accord and gave praises to God. In their language they said, "Puji, Tuhan! Terima Kaseh, Tuhan!" which meant, "Praise the Lord! Thank You, Lord!" These powerful words rose up to Heaven with a great roar. The praises of God's people filled the air, and this continued for hours!

After the people had praised the Lord in their own language for more than one hour, their language suddenly changed into unknown tongues. It sounded like the noise of water rushing through rocks. I leaned toward the pastor and asked him what they were saying. With great surprise, he said, "I can't understand what they are saying!"

As we spoke, the Holy Spirit filled that Presbyterian pastor, and he, too, began to speak in tongues. About two in the morning, I excused myself from the pulpit and left the service to go and get some rest.

The next day I learned that people had remained in the building, saturated with God's power and speaking in unknown tongues, until the morning. Over three hundred people were slain under the power of the Holy Spirit. Many had to be carried to their rickshaws and taxis to be taken to their homes. One lady was in the Spirit for two weeks, receiving many revelations and visions from God during that time. No hands had been laid on any of these people, nor had they received any teaching on the subject of the baptism of the Holy Spirit. They had come expecting a mighty visitation from God, and as their hearts were filled with praises and adoration to Jesus, He had sent a great outpouring of the Holy Spirit. Many men and women of God were raised up out of that revival and are still serving the Lord in various parts of the world today.

After the meetings in Malang, I was invited by an Indonesian military doctor, Dr. Bing, to hold some crusades in the town of Makassar, on the small Indonesian island of Sulawesi. Three Christian churches on the island had been burned down while the believers were worshipping inside. The churches continued under heavy threat of violence by rebels who were deeply opposed to Christianity. I stayed with Dr. Bing under heavy security, totally unaware, at the moment, of what was happening in that place.

The first night of our meetings, Dr. Bing had military police escort me to the church. Then, when I arrived, he had a group of Boy Scouts escort me into the building. At first, I thought I was just being given the red-carpet treatment. Little did I know that I was being protected from the ever-present rebels. The Lord kept this from me, not revealing the danger I was in, so that I would not be distracted. I thank God that the Lord was with me. Isaiah foretold:

When thou passest through the waters, I will be with thee; and through the rivers, they shall not overflow thee: when thou walkest through the fire, thou shalt not be burned; neither shall the flame kindle upon thee.
Isaiah 43:2

The meeting that night started with much prayer and supplication to God. After the message, I gave an altar call for salvation, and a large crowd of people surged forward. Bishop Tan was overcome with joy and began to weep, so that it was impossible for him to continue interpreting. I had to call for someone else to lead the people to Christ with the prayer of repentance, and the meeting ended with great victory.

Afterward, I was curious to know why Bishop Tan had been so overcome with tears. He said, "Brother Doss, had you been in my shoes, you would have done the same. Do you know there were over five hundred rebels in the building tonight? They came with the sole intention of disturbing our service. Almost every one of them came to the altar, repenting before God and giving their hearts to Jesus!" The prayer of his heart had been that even the rebels would see the glory of God and be converted, and God had honored his faith.

Many more wonderful things took place in Indonesia, for which I give God all the glory. As Fanny Crosby's great hymn says:

> *To God be the glory — great things He hath done!*
> *So loved He the world that He gave us His Son,*
> *Who yielded His life an atonement for sin,*
> *And opened the lifegate that all may go in.*

"To God Be the Glory" by Fanny J. Crosby.

CHAPTER 7

MY JOURNEY TO HONG KONG

Then spake the Lord to Paul in the night by a vision,
Be not afraid, but speak, and hold not thy peace: for I
am with thee, and no man shall set on thee to hurt
thee: for I have much people in this city.

Acts 18:9-10

On my return trip to the United States from Indonesia, the ship stopped for a few days at Manila, where I was invited to speak at a rally for Youth for Christ. I was then scheduled to speak for a banquet to be held by the Full Gospel Business Men's Fellowship International in Hong Kong. Its director, Mr. S.K. Sung, arranged a week of meetings at the Canadian Assembly of God church there, where Reverend Paul Kauffman was the pastor.

When I arrived in Hong Kong, Brother Sung took me straight to a prayer meeting at the church. As I walked into the auditorium, I saw it filled with Christians on their knees praying. I knelt down between two missionaries in the only space available. After the prayer, one of the missionaries invited me to speak in their churches in Hong Kong, Kowloon, the New Territories and Macau, a small Portuguese colony adjoining Communist China. They were small churches, but there were many of them.

A group of missionaries took me to Macau for a week of meetings. It was still nearly impossible to enter mainland China to proclaim the Gospel, and, in fact, many Chinese refugees were flooding into Hong Kong and Macau from the mainland. China's borders were heavily guarded by gunboats, and many refugees trying to escape from China through the water were shot to death. We were constantly watched by Communist soldiers from mainland China during our services, and spies commonly attended meetings during those days.

Because many physical healings occurred during the services in Macau, two doctors were sent from mainland China to find cause to arrest me on medical grounds. During the services, the Holy Spirit moved in the word of knowledge, revealing the sicknesses of the people and healing them as the prayer of faith was offered. The two doctors, who came to our meetings night after night, were moved by the power of God and were saved.

After a week of meetings, I was given a send-off Chinese dinner, a common practice in Southeast Asia. During that dinner, many people got up and testified of their healing. The two doctors were among them and gave glorious testimonies of their healing, salvation and deliverance. They also declared that most of their patients who were in the services had been totally healed. A Chinese author wrote a book of remembrance recounting the miracles and deliverances at these meetings, to give glory to God. Many wonderful works of the Lord are recorded in that book.

During the meetings in Hong Kong and Kowloon, a Canadian missionary, Sister Gwen Shaw, was inspired and challenged to launch out into a deeper ministry. I am privileged to be able to share her testimony here, and I pray that it may bless you as it has blessed me and many others:

THE TESTIMONY OF SISTER GWEN SHAW, THEN A MISSIONARY TO CHINA

"From the time I became a Christian, there was always a cry in my heart that God would use me. Even though I was a missionary, I felt unfulfilled. My 'work' left my soul dissatisfied, for I felt I was only treading a dry mill and that my ministry was unproductive. I was not sending forth the living water to the dry and thirsty land, as I felt I should.

"I dedicated my life to Christ immediately after my conversion and went to Bible college for three years. After a year of studying the Chinese language in the University of Toronto, Canada, I went as a 'faith' missionary to China. I had not had any opportunity to train for a secular profession, and perhaps this was best, for then I might have been tempted to fill the vacuum in my soul with some kind of earthly ambition.

"The years went by, and I 'served' God in my weakness, always reminded of my uselessness because I sensed a lack of anointing on my work for Him. Then one day God answered my prayer. He sent to our church a man who was anointed in a way I had never seen before. His name was Charles Doss. As he preached, I saw evidence of the miraculous power of God. Not only were the sick healed and church members blessed; their lives were transformed. I saw the quiet, dignified Chinese people fall prostrate in the presence of God's power.

85

Many did not arise for hours. They wept, shouted and praised the Lord. They were given visions of Heaven and Hell, the saints of the Bible, and the angels who serve us. When they stood up, they were transformed forever.

"I loved my people, and I had served them as a 'Spirit-filled' missionary for fourteen years, yet I saw God do more through this anointed servant in fourteen days than I had seen in my fourteen years of ministry. This was a visitation from God, and I wanted God to visit me in this way and use me to help to revive His Church. I began to wonder what was lacking in my life.

"I will never forget one of the days when Brother Doss was preparing to leave. Our whole church was going by boat to a small island near the China mainland to preach. A blind beggar boarded the boat, feeling his way along with a cane. In his trembling hand he held a tin cup which held his meager collection of small coins, the fruits of his begging. To my surprise, I saw our well-dressed evangelist go over and sit beside the beggar. He put his arm around him and began to speak, 'We are brothers, and I want to talk with you because I love you.'

"Tears came to my eyes. For an hour I watched as he tenderly told this man about the love of God and the sacrificial death of Jesus, His Son. Like the multitudes of others, this beggar had never heard that story before. Then and there, I wanted the same love from God that this evangelist had. I asked him this question: 'Brother, what is the secret of God's anointing in your life?'

"He smiled at me, and then, seeing my searching, earnest face, he got very sober and said to me, 'Sister, if you really want to know, I'll tell you.' He told me how he had been an evangelist in England with seemingly a lot of popularity and worldly success. But he realized that he did not have the true anointing of God, and so he sought God for this anointing.

"God told him to fast. 'And so,' he said, 'I fasted for thirty days, and I have never been the same since. There are two things I have done. I have given myself to God one hundred percent, and I have fasted.'

"Then I knew this is what had made him different. It was not enough to be baptized in the Holy Spirit and speak in tongues. We all did that, but we had so little fruit. We needed to pay a price. I determined I would pay that price in absolute commitment to the God of my life — at *all* cost. I would ask Him to give me a fast, a consecrated fast.

"For one year before that time, I had fasted one day a week, and it had been a great sacrifice for me to do this. I was doing it for those in the family who needed a miracle. I had never fasted for God to do something in me.

"Before our brother evangelist returned to his own country, I told him about my decision to fast. He warned me to be very careful about my motives. 'Keep your motives right. During a time of fasting, the devil will tempt you as he did Jesus. Be sure your heart is pure before God and that you are not fasting for any earthly gain. God will not honor that, and you will get into trouble.'

"I accepted his warning and asked for his prayers that God would keep me humble and hungry only for Him. The next day, after his departure, I knelt to pray and ask God to give me a specific time to fast. As I had often prayed, 'Teach me to pray,' I now asked Him, 'Teach me to fast.'

"I was a busy person. I had many responsibilities, and I needed strength. I knew little about fasting, only that I must keep my motives pure. As I prayed, God directed me to Daniel 10:2-3: *'In those days I Daniel was mourning three full weeks. I ate no pleasant bread, neither came flesh nor wine in my mouth, neither did I anoint myself at all, till three whole weeks were fulfilled.'* This was the fast God would give me — three weeks on liquids. I rejoiced greatly but remembered I was expecting someone to come that day. If they came, I knew I would not be able to fast. I put out my fleece: 'Lord, if it is Your will for me to fast now, give me these three weeks alone. Don't let my guest come.' A few hours later, a telegram arrived stating that my friend had been delayed for three weeks. I knew this was my appointment with God.

"Sometime near the end of the fast, God spoke to me, 'You think you know consecration, but that which you have consecrated is nothing in comparison to the complete yielding up of *all*. I want you to die — so you might live an abundant life — not a physical death, but die to all your carnal love, your desires, your needs, your longings, your dreams, your hopes, your plans. Die to the attractions of the eye, the appetites of food, the fleshly vanities of life — die! die! die!'

"Anything I have done, and anything God has done through my life, dates back to when God sent His servant Charles Doss to challenge me to fast. I kept my appointment with God. I paid a very small price, and the rewards are continuing. I know that these rewards will go on into eternity, for His anointing abides."

CHAPTER 8

SETTING CHURCHES ON FIRE FOR GOD

And they went forth, and preached every where, the Lord working with them, and confirming the word with signs following.   Mark 16:20

After my visit to Hong Kong in 1963, I returned to the United States to complete my commitments to the various churches where I had been forced to cancel meetings to make the Indonesian journey. The men of the Full Gospel Business Men's Fellowship International also kept me very busy ministering in their various chapters throughout Arizona. During these meetings, many denominations — including Methodists, Presbyterians, Lutherans and Baptists — opened up to the faith ministry.

While I was in Arizona, a church by the name of Gospel Echoes experienced a powerful visitation of the Holy Spirit. The pastor, Charles E. McHatton, kept in close touch with me during my ministry in Phoenix. He was so impressed by the gift of the word of knowledge that operated in my ministry that he was intent to learn more about it. We had lunch together several times. Even though he pastored a large and busy church, he followed me to various churches where I ministered. His desire was for the gifts of the Spirit to function in his ministry, especially the word of knowledge.

One cannot be taught to operate in the gifts of the Spirit. They function purely by the grace of the Holy Spirit and not by biblical knowledge, even though one can study about them. Paul wrote to the Corinthians:

But all these [gifts] worketh that one and the selfsame Spirit, dividing to every man severally as he will.
                                               1 Corinthians 12:11

Pastor McHatton was hungry to see the moving of God, so he invited me to hold an eight-day crusade in his church. The meetings held at Gospel Echoes were very fruitful. Many souls were converted, and miraculous healings took place in each service. An old man who was brought in on a stretcher with an oxygen tank to aid his respiration was totally healed. He discarded the oxygen cup from his nose and mouth, got up from his stretcher, and walked away. Some crippled people who were brought to the meeting in wheelchairs were healed and were able to walk without aid. The meetings were a great challenge, not only to that particular congregation, but to several ministers who came forward and rededicated their lives to be channels of blessing.

In our final service at Gospel Echoes, Pastor McHatton was greatly stirred by faith to take off his thick lenses, trusting God for total recovery of his eyesight. I have never since known him to wear those heavy lenses.

Seeing this remarkable move of God in his church encouraged him even more to seek after the gifts of the Spirit. At the close of the crusade, around midnight, he knelt down at the altar and rededicated his life for a deeper ministry. Since then, the Holy Spirit has taken him into a closer walk with God and has accomplished wonderful works through him in the state of Arizona and overseas. The word of knowledge has been very active in his ministry.

A short time later, Pastor Carl Holleman of Central Assembly of God Church in Phoenix asked me to speak in a series of meetings at his church. In those meetings, we saw many young people flock to the altar to seek the face of God night after night. The entire crusade was empowered with the Holy Spirit because of the hunger of the youth. One night, the platform was filled with young people, since there was no space in the sanctuary for them. Many people were converted and baptized in the Holy Spirit that night. Many miraculous things took place in the lives of the people of that church, and pastor Holleman declared that he had never seen such a moving of God in all his ministry.

One particular night the Holy Spirit prompted me to call a young woman by the name of Betty Britain up out of the audience to pray for her. Looking at her, I knew she was not accustomed to our type of meeting. To prepare her for what I was going to say to her, I asked her if she believed that I was a man of God. Betty said she did. "If I am able to tell you your physical ailment," I asked her, "would you believe that it was a word of knowledge from the Lord?" She said she would. Then I told her that everything was okay in her body except for her blood condition. Her expression changed because she was not aware of any such disorder in her body. I prayed for her anyway, because she expressed faith for her healing.

That night she went home and pondered the evening's events. A month before, she had undergone a medical checkup and had not yet gone back to her doctor for the results. When she went to the doctor's office the next day, the doctor used almost the same words I had used, "Everything shows up okay, except ..."

Betty interrupted him. "It's my blood condition, isn't it?"

Her doctor was surprised and asked her how she knew about it. Betty told the doctor about the meeting and how I had called her out through the word of knowledge and had ministered to her. She told him that she believed the Lord had healed her in that service. She had a second blood test that day, and it revealed that her blood was now normal. Both the doctor and the patient rejoiced together and gave God the glory!

One Thursday morning I was asked to visit a gentleman who had suffered a nervous breakdown some weeks before. Pastor Holleman accompanied me to the hospital where this gentleman had been admitted. He was a prominent businessman by the name of Mr. John Mull. John owned three sprinkler manufacturing companies in the Southwest, but he had incurred many problems in his business. Customers owed him hundreds of thousands of dollars, and he had been unable to collect the money. Facing financial ruin had led to his mental collapse.

As I walked into his private room at the Camelback Hospital, John asked me if I had come to convert him. I told him that nobody could convert him but God Himself. We sat together and talked a bit. As we talked, the Holy Spirit led me to ask him if he had ever broken a vow that he had made to God. John broke down and cried and admitted that he had. There had been a time, when his business was just beginning, that he made a vow that if God prospered him, he would go to church with his family and serve God the rest of his life. Even when he was not able to go to church, he would at least send his wife and children.

He had kept the vow for a while, and everything had gone well for him. His business prospered, and he and his family were happy.

At the height of his prosperity, however, John had begun to fail in his promise to God. He not only stopped going to church, but he hindered his wife and children from going. As he related all this to me, he broke down and wept bitterly.

The Holy Spirit led me to pray for John that he would repent and repay his vow. I assured him that if he did this, the Lord would restore to him all that he had lost. John sincerely prayed that day for Jesus to forgive him and to cleanse him from all his unrighteous living. He made a fresh commitment to serve God.

That same night, at the evening service, when I came onto the platform I noticed a well-dressed couple in the congregation, sitting near the aisle. During the altar call, they came right up front, close to the pulpit. The man reached out his hands and took mine. Gripping my hand firmly, he asked, "Do you remember me?"

I had to admit that I did not.

"I am John Mull," he told me, "the man you prayed for this morning at the Camelback Hospital."

The doctors had determined him to be healed and had discharged him from the hospital the very day he was prayed for. It was an instantaneous miracle.

Both John and his wife Fay gave their hearts to Jesus that night in full surrender, and John's life was totally changed. He came to my office one morning after his conversion and poured out his heart about his past life. He rejoiced to know that all had been changed. As the Scriptures declare:

> *Therefore if any man be in Christ, he is a new creature: old things are passed away; behold, all things are become new.* 2 Corinthians 5:17

I had the privilege of visiting John's factory in Phoenix the following week and had lunch with him. During our conversation, John confided in me that he had lost his temper many times with his debtors, and that some of them felt threatened by him because of his outbursts. I advised him to commit his ways to the Lord, since he had become His child. God was indeed his loving heavenly Father and would take care of all his needs. I quoted Jesus' words to him:

> *As many as received him, to them gave he power to become the sons of God, even to them that believe on his name.* John 1:12

Later, John noticed that as he committed his ways to the Lord, things began to change in his life, his family and his business. One day, a prominent doctor who was constructing a private hospital asked John to give him an estimate for installing a fire protection sprinkler system in the hospital. The doctor demanded an estimate immediately. John said that he would have to take the blueprints of the building back with him and study them. He would call the doctor back with an estimate. The doctor, however, was adamant. He demanded an immediate answer and he did it in a manner that previously would have greatly irritated John. In that moment, John remembered my words, that he was no longer on his own but that his heavenly Father would lead and guide him because he was saved and now a son of God. I was so proud to hear John testify later that he had not argued with the doctor. Instead, he testified to the doctor that he was no longer the same argumentative, temperamental John Mull, but a son of God, truly born again, and that God Himself would take care of his business as he trusted in Him.

The doctor had been overcome by his testimony. He pulled the blueprints from his drawer and thrust them into John's hands, saying, "Go ahead, John. Get it done and send me the bill!" This experience really spoke to John.

I later learned that he had been raised by a godly mother who was a well-known saint in the Church of God in Phoenix, and she had prayed often for her son's salvation. I had the privilege of fellowshipping with her before she went to be with the Lord. Mother Mull was well over ninety when she went home to be with the Lord. Before she closed her eyes, she held my hands and praised God for her son's salvation. We must never underestimate a mother's prayers.

CHAPTER 9

A MISSIONARY JOURNEY TO BRAZIL

And they brought unto him all sick people that were taken with divers diseases and torments, and those which were possessed with devils, and those which were lunatic, and those that had the palsy; and he healed them. Matthew 4:24

In 1965, Dr. Lester Sumrall phoned me from South Bend, Indiana, and asked if I would go to the city of Brasilia to preach and to direct a Bible school he was building there. He flew down to Phoenix and met me at a hotel to talk more about his ministry in Brazil and the possibility of my going there to serve with him. I was willing to meet him and discuss the matter, although I had never felt the Holy Spirit directing me to Bible school work. My calling had always been to serve as an evangelist, not an administrator.

I took this matter to my board of directors, a group of men God had given me to help with the work of Worldwide Harvester Crusade, Inc., and I explained to them that despite the fact that Dr. Sumrall had asked me to take the trip, he would not be responsible for me financially. The trip would have to be taken solely by faith, as before, not trusting in any human resources.

This proved to be a sore point with some of my directors, and some of them were very opposed to the idea. They had not been associated with my ministry long and wanted to know how such a trip could be taken without proper financing.

I was not deterred by this. By faith I called and made airline reservations. I did not have the funds for the airline ticket, but I knew that God was faithful. Soon afterward I received a phone call from a friend, Yule Britain. He was the husband of Betty, the young woman I had called up to the front in that meeting in Phoenix to give her the word of knowledge regarding her blood condition. As I reported in an earlier chapter, Betty was miraculously healed in that service. Now Yule was on the phone, offering to go with me to assist in my crusades in Brazil. I called the airline again and made a second reservation. To the glory of God, every single penny of our expenses during the entire trip — hotel, radio, television and travel — was paid by this gracious brother whom God had led to go with me. Glory be to our God!

In Brazil, we held three services a day, and every evening after the services I was on radio and television, broadcasting the good news of the Gospel of Jesus Christ. Miraculous healings took place in each service.

The practice of witchcraft is still very common in South America. During the crusades (which were held in a tent), many possessed with demon spirits would bark, howl and scream disruptively in the middle of the service. These people were gloriously set free from demon possession in the wonderful name of the Lord Jesus Christ!

The news of the meetings spread throughout the hotel where I was staying, and the staff of the hotel requested prayer for their needs. Many of them were saved as a result.

One particular morning, while I was resting, there came a knock at the door. Yule opened the door and revealed a large crowd of people standing outside. Most of them carried sick babies in their arms. Yule tried to stop them from entering the room, but they rushed through the door anyway. Some even threw their babies on my bed in desperation. Most of the babies were instantly healed, even before we had time to pray for them.

At the airport on the day we left Brazil for home, we were paged and requested to come to the office of one of the airlines. When we arrived, various airline staff members were waiting there to be prayed for. It was a strange and glorious sight to see the crowd follow us right to the steps of the airplane! How great is our God, anywhere and everywhere!

CHAPTER 10

A VISIT BACK HOME TO INDIA

*Fear not: for I am with thee: I will bring thy seed from
the east, and gather thee from the west.*   Isaiah 43:5

In 1967, the Holy Spirit led me to return to India for
ministry. The first city I visited was in the southwest, a
place called Kottayam, in the state of Kerala. I went there
totally by faith, not being invited by any church or organization. I had been told of a godly man who lived there
by the name of P.M. Philip, pastor of a full-Gospel church.
The Holy Spirit put it upon my heart to visit him, and
he gladly opened his home to me and invited me to stay
with him.

The day after I arrived in Kottayam, I opened my heart
to Pastor Philip and told him that I was led by the Spirit
to hold a mass crusade to reach souls for Christ in that
city. He was very interested in the idea, but when he set
about to reserve some public facility where we could
hold the campaign, he found that because it was elec-
tion time in the state, it did not seem to be a good time
for a crusade. For one thing, people were busy, so atten-
dance would not be good. Secondly, the party in power
in Kerala state at that time was the Communist Party of

India (CPI), and Communist flags were being prominently displayed in every public place. If we conducted a meeting on public grounds, we would be required to display the Communist flag too, he explained.

Despite these negative circumstances, I strongly felt that my visit to the city was in the perfect will of God, and I told the pastor this with strong conviction. Pastor Philip was convinced and came up with a solution. He arranged to hold a meeting for about two hundred people on the grounds outside his house.

The Spirit of God descended in great power in the very first service, and God manifested His healing might. Several deaf people were totally healed and, with great excitement, demonstrated their hearing. The word of knowledge operated so clearly that the small gathering was stirred with excitement. The following day, the crowd grew from two hundred to more than a thousand people. Fortunately, the pastor owned several acres of land surrounding his house, so he was able to accommodate the increased crowd.

The third day, there were more than three thousand people, both Christians and non-Christians, gathered all over the grounds. By the end of that week, many thousands had gathered to hear the Gospel. Pastor Philip was so excited by what God was doing that he was even willing to cut down acres of banana and pepper plants to accommodate the unexpected crowd. By this time, he was convinced that the Lord had indeed sent me, even though circumstances had appeared to be against us. This was a great lesson to all of us to obey the leading of God's Spirit, to be *Led by the Master's Hand* in everything that we do.

A Visit Back Home to India

The news of the meetings spread throughout India. In Vijayawada, in the state of Andhra Pradesh, Pastor Abraham Samuel was conducting a nationwide Gospel convention. When he heard of the success of the Kerala meetings, he sent a telegram, asking me to minister at the convention.

The purpose of the convention was to anchor Christians in the Word of God through teaching, but I was being led by God to hold evangelistic crusades, and not to minister to the people who were already saved. Since I was being led to preach salvation and win souls, I wrote back and declined the invitation. Pastor Samuel was determined to have me speak and made a great effort to persuade me to come to Vijayawada. Finally, I agreed to go if he would change the order of the convention and make it into a crusade to reach the lost. To my surprise, he agreed.

When I arrived in Vijayawada, I met several missionaries and businessmen from the United States who were also scheduled to speak at the convention. My coming to Vijayawada and changing the order of the meeting did not please some of them. At the first, this caused a heavy spirit of confusion and jealousy to dominate the atmosphere of the meetings. As I continued to pray and center my mind on the Lord, the Holy Spirit dealt with some of the men, and they came to me and repented of their wrong attitude and asked me to pray for them. One man of God was led by the Spirit to the terrace of the house where we were staying, there to wait on the Lord. He was dealt with by the Holy Spirit all through the night. The following morning he came to my room with tears of repentance and prayed with me for the will of God to be done in the meeting in Vijayawada.

Many hundreds of souls were gloriously converted in that crusade, and most of them were students of a nearby university. Among the students there were many Hindus. They not only were converted, but they had me speak at the university in their graduation ceremony. In this, we all saw the mighty hand of God.

The Scriptures are true:

> *For as many as are led by the Spirit of God, they are the sons of God.* Romans 8:14

At the conclusion of the meetings in Vijayawada, many hundreds were baptized in the river Godavari. I had the great blessing of baptizing my two older brothers, Albert and Richard Doss, along with other new converts.

Leaving Vijayawada, I traveled to Madras City, my hometown, where I preached for three days in another convention held by Pastor Abraham Samuel. Here, too, the Lord poured out an abundant blessing. One of the notable miracles which occurred in Madras was with a man who had elephantiasis in one of his legs. He was called out of the crowd through the word of knowledge.

The man was sitting at the back of the crowd of about twenty thousand people, when the Spirit of the Lord spoke through me and called him out, stating his condition very clearly. He came slowly and painfully through the vast crowd, dragging his hugely swollen leg. It took him a long time to get down to the altar.

Calling upon the name of the Lord Jesus Christ, I rebuked and cursed the disease in that man's leg, commanding it to leave. Outwardly, nothing appeared to happen, but the Holy Spirit assured me that he had been healed.

Many times people question me when I say to them, "You are healed in Jesus' name." Usually, the reason is that the sufferer does not see the result immediately. But when God speaks and assures healing, we must accept it by faith.

Many years later, when I was in Malaysia in 1978, an evangelist from India met me and asked me if I had been back to Madras since 1967. I told him I had not. He began to relate the healing of that man who had elephantiasis in his leg. Although I had not seen the leg being healed instantly, a year after the meeting the man's leg was completely restored and returned to normal size. This evangelist told me that people were talking about this miracle in Madras and were wondering if I would return for crusades. He urged me to go back, since there was great faith in the hearts of the people because of this miracle, and they were now very open to the Gospel.

Soon contacts were made with the churches in Madras, and preparations began for another mass crusade in that city. Many believers in India formed large prayer groups to fast and pray to prepare for the upcoming meetings. The crusade was well organized, with more than two thousand Spirit-filled counselors, men and women who were trained in spiritual guidance.

On June 8, 1980, we started the five-day crusade in a sports arena. It held twenty-five thousand people, but still people had to come early to be assured of a seat. The very first night of the meetings, about three thousand came to the altar to give their hearts to Jesus. While I was leading them to Christ in the prayer of repentance, I heard a commotion in the men's section. I opened my eyes and was surprised to see that a man who was seriously ill had fallen to the ground. I heard the people say that he was dead.

Behind the man were two doctors who had accompanied him because of his delicate health. I stepped down from the platform and looked toward the doctors. They shook their heads, indicating that the man was indeed dead. I wasn't about to accept that diagnosis. I wanted first to make sure that he was dead, and then I intended to pray for a miracle of life.

I laid my hands on the man's chest, calling upon the name of the Lord Jesus Christ to bring him back to life. At first, nothing appeared to happen. I held on to God, seeking earnestly for the return of the man's life. It took about fifteen or twenty minutes before I saw his eyelids begin to flutter. Then he opened his eyes and stared into space. The people around him who saw this were overcome with great surprise and excitement.

The man then got up and came running to the platform to testify of what had happened. Before he spoke, the two doctors who had been with him confirmed to the congregation that he had indeed been dead and, after prayer, had been restored to life.

The man himself gave a marvelous testimony. He said that while he was praying the sinner's prayer for salvation, he had suddenly blacked out. After a while he heard a soft voice saying, "Jesus, Jesus, Jesus." In reality, I had been praying to God with all my heart, shouting, and calling out the name of Jesus as loudly as I could, over and over again. It was these words that he heard, ever so softly, even though I was yelling them with all my strength.

He said that after he had heard the name of Jesus, he saw a flame of fire in the shape of an arrow soaring through the sky and piercing him right in the middle of his chest. His whole body became very warm, and then he woke up. Until that moment he had been a staunch Hindu and had never read the Bible or been to a Christian church in his life. The next day, he came to the service and gave another glorious testimony.

He told the congregation that he had spent thousands of rupees on medication and treatment for brain damage. Before the people's eyes, he voluntarily threw all the medication away and said, "I don't need these anymore since the Lord Jesus has healed me completely." He had been healed during the night, he said.

Then, while he lay in his bed, he heard a voice telling him to get up and write down a message. He quickly got up, found a piece of paper and a pencil, and wrote down what he had heard. These were the words:

Fear thou not; for I am with thee: be not dismayed; for I am thy God: I will strengthen thee; yea, I will help thee; yea, I will uphold thee with the right hand of my righteousness. Isaiah 41:10

He spoke this in his native language, Tamil, which happened to be my native language as well, and I was very excited because I had had a visitation from the Lord some months before taking this trip, and the Lord had given me the same promise.

On one of my missionary journeys, this one to Malaysia (I tell about it in the very next chapter), I had met a lovely lady, Grace Arthur, and in December of 1973 she became my wife. By now Grace and I had two lovely sons. Alex was five and Joshua was still an infant. Around midnight, on the second of January, 1980, I went out to a grocery store to purchase a few items for the family. While I was in the store, I was silently crying out to God to reveal Himself to me and to give me an assurance that I was in His perfect will in the ministry. After many years of serving Him, I still was not satisfied with what I was doing for my Lord. My desire had been to lead at least a million souls to Christ, and by this time, I had already won more than four hundred thousand men and women to Him. Still, there was an insatiable desire in my heart to do more.

When I got back to the house, Grace asked me if I would read Alex a bedtime story. She was putting Joshua to sleep in the other bedroom.

After Alex had gone to sleep, I was lying next to him, just dozing off, when suddenly I felt a very strong presence in the room. I was not frightened by it, since the experience was so peaceful. I did, however, look down at the floor because of the reverence I felt for this manifestation. As I did, the entire carpet appeared white with the brightness in the room, although it was, in reality, a bright gold and blue shag. As the bright light intensified, I looked up and saw Jesus standing beside me.

His raiment was a beautiful white, and the folds of His garment were tinged with a faint, soft blue. He had his right hand folded, and His lily-white robe flowed over His arm. I was awestruck and quickly closed my eyes, but I could still see Him. His gracious eyes looked straight into me and penetrated my soul with love and encouragement, assuring me that He was with me and that what I was doing was His perfect will.

While Jesus looked at me, He spoke these words, "I am Jesus; I am alive; and I am alive forevermore. You are doing My will, proclaiming My resurrection. Fear not, I am with you to strengthen you to declare the message."

While Jesus was speaking to me, I saw myself with my knees against my chest in a fetal position, and I was in the midst of a flaming fire. Still, I was not burned. Then, just as suddenly as He had come, the Lord disappeared.

When I came to myself, I was shaking from the effect of this visitation. I quickly got up and ran to the other room to tell Grace what had happened. Usually, she left the door open, but it was shut this time. As I was about to open it, the enemy tried to tell me that I should not mention this experience to my wife. She might not believe me. I ignored this advice and opened the door.

I found Grace sitting up in bed. When I told her that I had seen Jesus, she immediately cried out, "I believe it! I believe it!" Although she had not seen Him, she, too, had felt the presence of the Lord in the house. She said that she had actually left the door of her room open, but it closed by itself. She had not been frightened by this. We agreed that a heavenly manifestation had come to our home.

Both of us went down to Alex's room, knelt at the spot where the Lord had appeared and surrendered our lives afresh to His service. After a while, I went into the living room and opened the Bible to see what the Lord would say to me through His Word. The Bible opened to Isaiah 41, and verse 10 seemed to be illuminated before me.

I had had a similar experience in 1962, while preaching among the Mennonites in Huntsburg, Ohio. I had found myself growing very weary from the long hours of ministry and lack of opportunity to rest. One night, as I lay in bed, my body aching, I had cried out to God and asked Him to strengthen me. About two in the morning, I saw Jesus coming into my room. He reached out His hand and held mine in His. I was soon out of the bed, walking with Him to the entrance of the room, where He disappeared. While my hand had been in His, my entire body was charged with supernatural strength. I quickly turned the light on and opened the Bible to see what the Lord would say to me through His Word. Again, Isaiah 41:10 became illuminated before my eyes, and I received supernatural strength from the Lord.

After twice seeing the vision of Christ and hearing the man who was raised from the dead bring the same message, I could never doubt that Christ is alive today, and so is His wonderworking power. I strongly believe in the strength of the right hand of His righteousness. I was amazed to hear this man, whom the Lord had raised from the dead, share this very scripture which the Lord had spoken to me before.

After his testimony, thousands lined up to be prayed for. One teenage girl who was a deaf-mute came for healing. She was instantly healed and was able to hear people whispering behind her. She was also able to speak clearly.

The next day, this girl came to the crusade to demonstrate her healing. She took the microphone and sang fluently the song "I'm So Glad Jesus Set Me Free." Her singing was taped as a living testimony of God's healing power. The Bible says that dumb tongues shall sing praises unto our God. We indeed saw the dumb tongue singing praises to His Holy name.

Since then, we have seen many deaf-mutes healed and given the ability to sing. In Malaysia alone, more than eighty deaf-mutes spoke, heard and sang praises to the Lord. Medical doctors were at the altar as counselors and were able to examine those who claimed healing. They found them to be supernaturally healed.

During the five-day crusade in Madras, more than ten thousand people gave their hearts to Jesus Christ. The majority of them had been Hindus. All glory and honor and praise go entirely to our Lord Jesus Christ!

CHAPTER 11

LED BY THE SPIRIT
TO MALAYSIA

*For as many as are led by the Spirit of God, they are
the sons of God.*   Romans 8:14

I first went to Malaysia in 1973. Ostensibly my trip
was to visit some of my relatives who lived in the town
of Klang, but, as usual, God had other reasons for my
going. One Sunday afternoon, I was resting in my aunt's
house when the Spirit urged me to get up and walk
downtown. I was then led by the Spirit to a gas station
owned by a Malaysian, a Moslem. I asked him if he could
direct me to a Christian church. To my great surprise, he
went and got his Rolls Royce out of the garage and drove
me to an Assemblies of God church he knew of and left
me there.

I knocked on the door of the church, and the pastor's
wife answered. I explained to her that I was a mission-
ary from the United States visiting the country and that
I had been led by the Holy Spirit to come to her church.
She quickly called her husband, Pastor Andrew Wong.
Pastor Wong graciously welcomed me into his study.

Led by the Spirit to Malaysia

During our conversation he related to me his dilemma. Some Australian missionaries had been scheduled as guest speakers in a series of weekend meetings in his church, but for some reason, they had failed to arrive. He didn't know quite what to do.

As we spoke, Pastor Wong recognized the provision of the Lord in sending me to his doorstep, and without us even knowing each other, he immediately opened the pulpit to me to minister on the weekend in his church.

From the very beginning, the meetings were blessed. The Lord worked wonders in the lives of the people who attended.

At the end of those weekend meetings, Pastor Wong, with great excitement, asked me if I would be willing to continue the services for another week, and I consented. The good news from the services spread, not only in the town of Klang, but throughout the neighboring communities as well. Other ministers opened their churches for special meetings, and, very soon, doors were opened in other parts of Malaysia for larger crusades in town halls and public auditoriums.

Pastor Henry Ramaya, a young preacher with Grace Assembly of God Church, was very active among the youth. He approached me to help him reach out to the students in Klang. He was able to arrange meetings in high schools, where we saw many students give their hearts to the Lord. These young people became zealous members of his church, and the church, which previously had just a handful of members, now quickly began to overflow with hundreds of new converts.

Each time I took a missionary journey to Malaysia, I held special healing crusades for Pastor Ramaya, and today Grace Assembly of God has grown so much that they were forced to move into a theater building. I had the privilege of praying over that building for years before it became available to the church.

Pastor Ramaya has arranged many meetings for me in Malaysia, mostly in small towns where few others have ministered. Thousands of Hindus, Buddhists and others have been converted and brought into the Kingdom of God through these meetings.

Of all the countries I have been to, Malaysia is the second nation where I literally laid down my life and came to the point of physical collapse, to win the lost and the dying with the Gospel of the Lord Jesus Christ. The first had been in Jamaica, as I reported in a previous chapter, where I preached for an entire year with only one day off. It seemed necessary at the time, because of the great harvest being reaped.

It was the many miracles of physical healing that stirred the interest of the Hindus, Buddhists and nominal Christians of Malaysia. In Kuala Lumpur people came forward with various bondages, and they were set free from their addictions. In the city of Petaling Jaya, we saw notable miracles. People afflicted with cancer were healed, and many who were confined to wheelchairs, stretchers and crutches were made whole and walked home without aid.

One lady, who had been bedridden for eight years with terminal cancer, was instantly healed. She had been unable to eat, sit or walk and had been given up by her doctors. They had said that she had no more than a month to live. We saw the power of God manifested in this hopeless case. After the prayer of faith in Jesus' name, this woman stood up and walked all over the platform. She even joined me in praying for others.

For twenty-six years now we have been visiting Malaysia with the Gospel of deliverance and have seen many churches spring up throughout this nation. In 1987, I was invited to Butterworth, a town near Penang Island, to hold some crusade meetings with the churches of the Assemblies of God. Proper police permits were secured for meetings in Butterworth and other parts of Malaysia as well.

In the first meeting in Butterworth, an outstanding physical miracle took place. A little girl, about four years old, was deaf and mute. She was born with only a stub of muscle in her mouth for a tongue. The Holy Spirit led me to touch her lips in Jesus' name, and then I asked her to speak the words "I love Jesus, and Jesus loves me."

There were hundreds of people at the altar watching this scene, as she opened her mouth and spoke out in fluent English, "I love Jesus, and Jesus loves me." Her mother, who was standing by her side, was overcome with excitement. She picked the girl up, ran outside of the building, and opened the child's mouth to look at it in better light. She found a complete tongue in her daughter's mouth.

The pastor of the church went out to examine the child and came back to testify to the miracle on the platform. The news of it spread not only throughout the town of Butterworth, but into the surrounding communities, and it drew many to hear the Gospel. In one church, more than eighty deaf-mutes were miraculously healed, and most of them could not only hear and speak, but could sing praises to God. These miracles of healing were confirmed by medical doctors who were present in the meetings.

Sometime later, I was requested to visit a man in the hospital who had gangrene in his leg and was scheduled to have it amputated. When I walked into his room, I found that he was full of fear, thinking about losing his leg the next day. The Lord gave me a wonderful opportunity to share the Gospel with him.

He was a churchgoer, having attended a Methodist church all his life, but he had never received Christ as his personal Savior and Lord. I opened the book of Isaiah to chapter 53 and read the entire chapter to him. The Holy Spirit spoke to his heart very clearly that Jesus, the Son of God, was indeed wounded for *his* transgressions and bruised for *his* iniquities and the chastisement of *his* peace was upon Him, and with His stripes *he* was healed:

> *He was wounded for our transgressions, he was bruised for our iniquities: the chastisement of our peace was upon him; and with his stripes we are healed.* Isaiah 53:5

The man began to weep with deep conviction of his sins and his need of a Savior. As I asked him to open his heart to the Lord, I accidentally touched the leg which had been totally numb. He jumped up because he had felt my hand touch his formerly lifeless leg. The entire room was filled with the presence of God!

The following day the doctors came into the room to prepare the man for surgery, but he insisted that they reexamine him, since he could now use his leg and believed that he had been healed. After a thorough examination, the doctors were convinced that there would be no need for the amputation. Jesus Christ was glorified in Malaysia through this and many other miracles. To God be the glory!

CHAPTER 12

CAMPUS MINISTRIES
IN THE UNITED STATES,
CANADA, JAPAN AND GERMANY

*And this gospel of the kingdom shall be preached in
all the world for a witness unto all nations; and then
shall the end come.*   Matthew 24:14

In the early eighties, a Christian businessman here in
Scottsdale urged me to hold some special meetings lo-
cally to teach faith. After praying much about it, I felt
that it was the right thing to do. We met every Tuesday
night, and the first few weeks a few people who were
hungry to learn more of God's Word and the life of faith
joined us. Then, very soon, the crowd began to build.
One particular Tuesday night, a fine group of vibrant-
looking young people came, and they continued to
attend our services and to prosper spiritually. I learned
that they were from Arizona State University, and before long, we found ourselves getting involved in
campus ministries there. I was invited to the campus
several times to preach to the students, and many of

them, both Americans and those from other nations, were saved and filled with the Holy Spirit at those campus meetings. That was just the beginning of a long and fruitful relationship with campus ministries.

A few months after this, I learned of an organization called the Maranatha Campus Ministries International, whose founder and director was Bob Weiner. During the month of December 1982, I was invited to a Christmas banquet the organization held at Arizona State University. There I met Reverend Wesley Steeleburg, and he invited me to attend the national convention of Maranatha Campus Ministries in Dallas, Texas.

In Dallas, I was introduced to Bob Weiner, and he urged me to help Maranatha Campus Ministries with the program of evangelism worldwide. I was deeply impressed with the zeal the young people of this ministry had for soul-winning on campuses everywhere, and as an evangelist with a burning passion for souls, I was ready to do whatever was necessary to encourage and build up others to win souls for Christ. In the coming months I was introduced to Maranatha churches throughout the United States, Canada and Europe.

The first meeting I held with these churches was in Eugene, Oregon. The three-day outreach in Eugene stirred the young people to reach the lost with great zeal. The meetings lasted until the early hours of the morning. The last service in Eugene was so powerful that the young people were afraid to close the service, not wanting to do anything to quench the revival fire. They were so afraid they would stop the flow of the Spirit that they called the Maranatha headquarters in Gainesville, Florida, to find out what to do. Since I was scheduled to go on to another Maranatha meeting, this one in Seattle, Washington, I had to leave them.

In Seattle, the power of the Holy Spirit was demonstrated, but because the pastor of the church was rather skeptical that what was happening was of God, he was slow to step into it, and the scheduled meetings came to an end.

After the final Sunday morning service, I was scheduled to leave for Vancouver, British Columbia, where another outreach would begin on Tuesday. That day at lunch, however, the pastor opened up his heart to me. He said he had come to realize that he was missing out on God's blessings because of his unbelief, and he asked if I would pray for him. He had been very skeptical, he said, of what actually occurred when people were "slain under the power of the Holy Spirit." There were many questions in his mind about the validity of such manifestations, and because of this he had drawn back and had not allowed the Holy Spirit to take over his services.

It was evident that despite his struggles he was really hungry for the sovereign move of God in his church, and this was proven when he asked me if I would stay one more night and pray that a double portion of God's Spirit would be imparted upon his congregation. I agreed.

Several hundred people gathered that night. At the outset of the service, the entire congregation got on their knees and repented before God. Confessing their faults also one to another, they asked forgiveness of each other and prayed for each other. As the people did this, the Holy Spirit began to manifest His presence. I spoke for thirty or forty minutes, and then the Lord took over the rest of the service in an unusual and supernatural way.

Many college football players came to the altar. Physically, they were giants. As the power of the Lord fell upon all those who were prayed for, they began falling like tall oak trees and lay prostrate on the floor under the power of God. Even before I could get to some of them, they were overcome by the power of God's presence and were saturated with the Spirit.

The meeting went from six in the evening right through to six the next morning. For twelve solid hours, the Holy Spirit had these young people under His influence. Young people were weeping all over the building, while others were laughing in the Spirit.

The pastor remained close to me during this time, expecting something to happen in his own life. About ten that night, he cried out to me, asking me to lay hands on him for a double portion of God's empowering in his life. Before I could touch him, he fell under the power of God and remained there for eight hours in the presence of God. How glad I was that I had stayed for the extra service!

In Vancouver, British Columbia, the people, although they were anxious to see the manifestation of God's power, were concerned about the emotional outbursts that could ensue. As soon as I met the pastor of the church, he warned me that they were Canadians and that what was acceptable in the United States might not be in Canada. I took his advice seriously and was very careful about how I ministered. The more careful I was, however, the less anointing I felt. During the final night, the pastor recognized that it is *"not by might, nor by power, but by [His] Spirit"* that God moves. He, too, repented of his carnal way and let the mind of the Lord have control in that last service.

I must say that I have never seen people get as excited as those Canadians! The Holy Spirit tore down all their formalities and religiosities and swept through that service in the mighty manifestation of His presence.

The young people in the service were stirred by the power of God's love, and some of them went right to their campuses after the service, stirring up other Christian young people and witnessing to the unsaved. The church in Vancouver will never forget the moving of God that took place in 1982.

Although all of those meetings were notable, news of what God had done in the Seattle meeting spread throughout Maranatha Campus Ministries in many counties, and invitations began pouring into our office. As the Lord led us, we scheduled many other outreach meetings.

My contribution to the Maranatha Campus Ministries was to demonstrate love and compassion in the Body of Christ. Everywhere I went, there was a great need for such ministry. The power of the Holy Spirit is the agape love of God, and college students were very attracted to the love of Jesus, as it flowed freely like a river in every service I held for the group. Hundreds of university students and, in some places, even professors, were saved and filled with the Holy Spirit. Many of those are now in the ministry, and many have been sent out as missionaries.

In 1988 I was invited by Brother Weiner to a leadership seminar in Gainesville, Florida, and asked to teach on the subject "Power for the Miraculous." Leaders of the organization from various parts of the United States and abroad who gathered at this seminar were expecting to hear teachings on healings and miracles and the power to have such ministry in their lives. The Holy Spirit, however, led me very clearly to teach them the love of God, which is the key to every successful Christian ministry. Love is the power for the miraculous. Winning lost souls is the miracle of all miracles, and it requires the power of God's love to accomplish it. Then signs, wonders and miracles will follow those who believe.

David sang:

> *Surely goodness and mercy shall follow me all the days of my life.*   Psalm 23:6

The teaching I gave at the leadership seminar was strongly based on the power of the Holy Spirit. Jesus said:

> *But ye shall receive power, after that the Holy Ghost is come upon you: and ye shall be witnesses unto me both in Jerusalem, and in all Judea, and in Samaria, and unto the uttermost part of the earth.*   Acts 1:8

Here, the Lord emphasized the power of the Holy Spirit and not the gifts — even though the gifts of the Spirit do follow the power of the Holy Spirit. What kind of power is Jesus speaking about? Love is the power of the Holy Spirit. It is possible to have all the nine gifts of the Holy Spirit operate in one's life and still lack His power. We experience the lack of such power in the Body of Christ today, and we need that power to win the world for Christ.

At the conclusion of my segment of the seminar, a mighty outpouring of the Holy Spirit came in the service. Many ministers realized, for the first time in their lives, what was lacking in their ministries. At the altar call, the Holy Spirit fell upon hungry young leaders and filled them with great love, and there we experienced waves of joy and laughter for hours. Many left the seminar with fresh revelation and vision for their ministry.

CHAPTER 13

MIRACLES TAKE US TO JAPAN

I will instruct thee and teach thee in the way which
thou shalt go: I will guide thee with mine eye.
                                                    Psalm 32:8

When God leads a person to a given country with a certain mission, He will provide the needed resources. It became my habit, whenever I took overseas trips, to calculate the amount of money needed and to mention it to my family, and to no one else. As a family, we prayed together for the specific amount we needed, and we left the rest with God.

A couple of weeks before my trip to Japan, I knelt with my family and prayed for a ten-thousand-dollar miracle, enough to pay for the trip and all my existing financial obligations at home. We prayed only once and believed that we had received what we asked for (see Mark 11:22-24).

A few days later, I was invited to Independence, Missouri, to preach to a small gathering of people in an independent church. Night after night, the people in the church were enthralled by the teaching of faith. On the last night, the Holy Spirit spoke to the pastor of the church concerning my need. This man did not know a single thing about our financial needs, and we never mentioned them to him. We had only mentioned financial needs to our heavenly Father and to each other within the family.

As I finished preaching that last night, the pastor got up and asked me to remain on the platform. He had something to say to me. He said that he had enjoyed the teaching every night, but this night he could not concentrate on anything I said. Over and over in his mind, he kept hearing the words "Ten thousand, ten thousand, ten thousand," and he could not understand what that meant. About the time I was to leave the platform, the Lord spoke to him, telling him to give me $10,000 to go to Japan and Malaysia and win souls for His Kingdom.

The young congregation had been saving money for the extension of their Christian school, but the pastor announced to them that he was now led to take money out of the building fund for the winning of lost souls in Japan and Malaysia. That very night he wrote a check for $10,000 for my trip.

The Lord is faithful and never denies His faithfulness. With miracles like this one, He supplies all our needs *"according to His riches in glory by Christ Jesus."*

We took the missionary journey to Japan and Malaysia in 1984, as planned, and when we returned, we received a praise report from the pastor in Independence, Missouri. Within a year, the Lord had supplied all the needs of the congregation, and a school building with a huge gymnasium had been completed debt-free. As the givers, those people received their part of the miracle.

In Japan, we spoke at the campus ministries in Tokyo,

where more than fifty Japanese professors had been invited to the meeting. Many wonderful miracles of healing and deliverance took place in all the services, and more than half of the professors gave their hearts to Jesus. The rest called us back and thanked us for inviting them to what they called "the love meeting."

Japan is a hard mission field, and I have found that it takes more than signs, wonders and miracles to win the Japanese people. It takes God's love. Not only Japan, but the whole world is starving for the genuine love of God, which only His redeemed Church can offer.

A young lady who was a follower of Mr. Moon of the Unification Church attended one of the services. Through the word of knowledge, I was able to point out to her the deception in her belief. At first she was reluctant to accept what I said, but the power of the Holy Spirit worked in her heart, and she came forward to surrender her life to Christ.

After leading her to Christ, I was about to pray for His leading in her life. Just before I began praying, evil spirits began to manifest themselves in her through abnormal physical symptoms, but, praise be to God, she was totally delivered, saved and filled with the Holy Spirit. What a victory it was! And it happened because of the power of Jesus' name and His blood.

A year before this trip, my wife and I, together with our three sons, had been on our way to Malaysia by way of Japan and had stopped overnight in Tokyo to make our connection to Malaysia the following morning. Arriving in Tokyo about nine in the evening, we checked into a hotel for the night. Early the following morning we went back to the airport for our connecting flight to Malaysia.

When we approached customs, we were told that we would have to pay an airport tax in the amount of 10,000 yen (approximately $50 US). Since we were transit passengers, I had not considered the need to pay an airport tax. I did not have a single yen in my pocket, and there were no banks open yet to exchange American dollars. While I was debating with the officer about the need to pay the tax, I was checking through my pockets, pretending to look for the money. When I looked into my topcoat pocket, I felt a roll of paper that had not been there before. I pulled it out and unrolled it, and the customs officer declared, "That's all we need." It was exactly 10,000 yen!

Throughout my years of ministry, I have seen many creative miracles. God is not only able to raise the dead. He is able to make things that did not previously exist miraculously appear, as they did in Bible days. The Scriptures are true:

> *Jesus Christ the same yesterday, and to day, and for ever.* Hebrews 13:8

CHAPTER 14

MIRACLES IN MUNICH

Then the eyes of the blind shall be opened, and the
ears of the deaf shall be unstopped. Then shall the lame
man leap as an hart, and the tongue of the dumb sing.
Isaiah 35:5-6

During our meeting in Munich, Germany, in 1985, many refugees from Sri Lanka were present, including many Hindus. The first night of our crusade, every one of the refugees who were there came forward for salvation, along with a number of German students.

As usual, after every salvation altar call, we proceeded with prayer for healing. One young man from Sri Lanka was a deaf-mute. He could only read lips and understand sign language. After the prayer for deliverance, he was totally healed and able to hear the very whisper of my words, and he spoke fluently. The following night he sang "I'm So Glad Jesus Set Me Free," giving glory to Jesus.

The German people are, for the most part, a very stern, unemotional people with strict self-discipline, but when they saw a genuine manifestation of God's power they became very excited and praised God. Every single night in Munich there was a great outburst of praise, due to God's infinite presence. Out of the German fellowship, many disciples were raised up for the ministry of the Gospel of Jesus Christ.

I love Germany very dearly, and it is my desire to return there for greater crusades in the future.

CHAPTER 15

A LONG-ANTICIPATED
JOURNEY TO SWEDEN

*Heaven and earth shall pass away; but my words shall
not pass away.* Luke 21:33

During my theological training at the Bible College
of Wales, I mentioned to one of the Swedish students
that one day I would be ministering in Sweden. That, of
course, was in the early fifties. It would be more than
thirty years before this great burden, placed on my heart
by the Holy Spirit, would become a reality.

As I began thinking about making a trip to Sweden, I
mentioned my plans to my wife, as I always sought her
agreement. Sometimes she felt a check in her spirit and
warned me not to proceed with my plans. This time, she
readily agreed and encouraged me to go, so we were
sure it was the will of God.

I had no personal invitation from Sweden, and I had
no money to go either. But just as soon as I felt the re-
lease of the Holy Spirit for the journey, I called a travel
agency in Los Angeles and made an airline reservation
for Stockholm, Sweden. The agent graciously made all

the necessary arrangements and mailed me the round-trip ticket. The cost for it was more than $1,300, and even after I had received the ticket, I had no money to pay it.

About a month went by, and I had still not received the finances for the ticket. About a week later, a sister all the way from Columbus, Ohio, appeared at our doorstep in her white Lincoln Continental. As she walked into our home, she said that her entire family had decided together to give us the car. The first thought that came to me was that I needed $1,300 for the airline ticket, not a car. The Holy Spirit quickened to me the words of Jesus:

> *But seek ye first the kingdom of God, and his righteousness; and all these things shall be added unto you.*
> Matthew 6:33

The phrase *"all these things shall be added unto you"* came to me as a fresh revelation from God. God adds and never subtracts. The added blessings of God were like a bonus to me.

When King Solomon was given the great task of ruling the children of Israel, he prayed that God would give him wisdom and knowledge to rule the nation well. He could have asked for material things — more and better armor or horses or camels to strengthen his army. Instead, he asked for God's wisdom and understanding. When God saw Solomon's righteous motives, He was pleased and blessed him, not only by giving him wisdom and knowledge, but also by making Solomon the richest king on Earth. King Solomon had been seeking the Kingdom of God and His righteousness, and the Lord had added wealth as a bonus.

This revelation blessed my heart. When we seek God's Kingdom and His righteousness first, the Lord not only meets our needs, but also gives us His blessings over and above them — as a bonus. I call this truth "an added blessing."

The sister from Ohio stayed with us overnight, and the following morning, at the breakfast table, she asked us if we were ready for another blessing. Knowing that the Lord often surprises me with His good gifts, I said we were ready. She unzipped a plastic bag and emptied its contents onto the table. It was a pile of money. There were twenties, tens, fives and one-dollar bills and much change. The Lord was meeting all my needs *according to His riches in glory by Christ Jesus.* After counting the money, we discovered that there was $1,300 and some change, the exact amount needed to pay the ticket!

When I went to the post office later that day, I found in the mail the invoice from the travel agency. God is always on time, never too early, nor too late. He is a present help at the moment of our need.

Two days before my flight to Sweden, I decided to take Grace and the boys on a fishing trip to spend some quality time with them before I left. Excitedly, they prepared to go, their faces alight with joy at the prospect of this treat.

Later that day, when I leaned over to wash my face, my back suddenly felt like it was splitting, and a searing pain spread over my lower back, so that I could barely stand. Soon I found myself lying on the floor in agonizing pain. The enemy had attacked me, but I was determined to get up and prepare for our special trip.

It was not easy, but as painful as it was, I was not about to give up my plan to take my family out for fellowship. We went, but for two solid days and nights, I experienced incapacitating pain. Grace gave me heatpad treatments and rubbed ointment into the muscles to relieve the pain, but my misery increased by the hour.

When we returned to our home in Scottsdale, I went to see my doctor in the hope that he could discover what was wrong with my back. After taking X-rays, the doctor had to say that he could not find anything wrong with me. He suggested that something might be telling me not to go on this upcoming trip. My answer to him was that Someone Else had told me to go, and I must obey the first command. He knew exactly what I meant, since he knew of my faith in God. He still suggested that I might want to postpone the trip.

I had to go. Faith is obedience, and obedience is faith. Jesus told a parable of two builders and two foundations:

> *Therefore whosoever heareth these sayings of mine, and doeth them, I will liken him unto a wise man, which built his house upon a rock: and the rain descended, and the floods came, and the winds blew, and beat upon that house; and it fell not: for it was founded upon a rock. And every one that heareth these sayings of mine, and doeth them not, shall be likened unto a foolish man, which built his house upon the sand: and the rain descended, and the floods came, and the winds blew, and beat upon that house; and it fell: and great was the fall of it.* Matthew 7:24-27

A Long-Anticipated Journey to Sweden

Real faith is obeying the Word of God. I had to go.

The Apostle James wrote that faith without obedience is just as dead as a body without the spirit. When God commands us to do something, we must obey Him. As we continue to respond to Him in obedience, the faith of God will be built up in our spirits.

A wise man is the one who, after hearing the Word of God, obeys and does what God is commanding. The Lord likened him to a man who built his house upon a rock (a solid foundation) which could not be moved. The rain descended, the floods came, and the winds blew and beat upon that house, but since the house was rooted and grounded upon a rock (obedience), it was not destroyed.

In my case, the Lord commanded me to go to Sweden, and I obeyed by making all the preparations. It was totally by faith, and my faith was tried by the enemy. He was attempting to stop me from advancing in obedience. The rain came down, and the floods came up, and the winds blew. Eventually, I was flat on my back, in agonizing pain. I had determined, however, to obey at any cost, and the pain and the misery it caused would not stop me — despite the doctor's recommendations to the contrary. The Lord wanted me to go at His appointed time, and I had to obey.

At Sky Harbor Airport in Phoenix a wheelchair was waiting for me. From the time I left Phoenix until I arrived in Stockholm, I was graciously assisted by a member of the airline staff, who took me from one gate to another in a wheelchair. While I was sitting in the wheelchair, rolling from gate to gate, the enemy tried to intimidate me with all sorts of accusations. I was tempted to feel sorry for myself, but the Holy Spirit reminded me that I was a privileged person, getting to travel in such comfort, not even having to walk or carry any hand luggage. Soon I felt as though I were being carried to the mission field in a comfortable chariot, and I rejoiced.

After clearing customs and immigration in Stockholm, I was wheeled outside the airport and left alone. The man who rolled me out there told me this was as far as he could take me. From there on, I was on my own.

So, there I was, sitting in a wheelchair outside the Stockholm Airport, not knowing a single soul, and not able to get up and walk anywhere. After a few minutes, a taxi drove up, and the driver asked if I needed a ride. He assisted me into the car, and I asked him to take me to a hotel close to the largest church in Stockholm. He took me to the Carlton Hotel, which was near City Church. I was assisted to my room on the fifth floor, where I stayed for four nights, spending the time flat on my back in agony.

I could not rest because of the persistent pain, so I passed the time praying. Nothing, however, seemed to relieve the pain.

On the fifth day, I was improved enough to get up, and the Holy Spirit led me to take a walk to the shopping center in Stockholm. As I limped through the streets, I came to a chandelier shop. I was drawn to the beauty of the crystal in the window, and after staring at it for a while, I was led to go inside. A young blond man standing behind the counter was the only person there. Not being sure that he could speak English, I pulled out a brochure, "Led by the Master's Hand," and handed it to him.

With a bright smile, he read it and then asked, "Are you a minister?"

"Yes, I am," I said. "Are you a Christian?"

In great excitement he replied, "Yes, I am a Christian!"

At that moment, two customers walked in and, with another flashing smile, my host excused himself to go and wait on them.

I stood rubbing my painful back and waiting for him to come back. As I waited, a well-dressed man walked through the doorway and stood with his briefcase in his hand. He stared questioningly at me. As I looked back at him, the Spirit of the Lord spoke out of my mouth with these words, "Thou art the man! God sent you my way for revival in Sweden! Your name is Bengt!"

When the man heard me, a total stranger, say his name, he turned to the young man I had been speaking with and asked him in Swedish, "Son, what did he say?" Apparently, he did not understand English.

The boy replied, "Father, he called you by your name and said you are the man that God sent his way for revival in Sweden."

At this point, Bengt was stirred. He came running to me saying, "*Yo! yo!* [Yes! yes!], *Pris be Gud!* [God be praised!]" and gave me a big hug and a holy kiss on my neck. As soon as he did that, the pain in my back instantly left me, and I heard the voice of God say, "You have kept My appointment and obeyed My voice; therefore My Spirit is upon you for revival in Scandinavia."

Brother Bengt turned and said to his son, "Mikkel, tell my brother that I have been praying all day long for God to send a messenger my way. I have invited over fifty guests to my home to minister to them. Most of them are at the verge of giving up either in their marriages or in business, and none of them is a Christian."

I spent that night in Bengt's home, ministering to some of the most needy people in Stockholm. The manifestation of God's grace and mercy was so strong that many were overcome by the power of God and were saved and delivered. The next day, the news of these wonderful events spread to the one and only Christian television station, which also published a daily Christian newspaper called *Dagen*, meaning *Today*. The director of the company interviewed me and gave full-page coverage of my visit to Sweden.

Everywhere I went for meetings, the director of that station followed me, gathering news and taking pictures to publish in the Christian newspaper. Within two weeks of my stay in Sweden, the news had spread throughout Scandinavia. We had people attending our crusades from Norway, Denmark, Finland and even Poland.

While I was in Sweden, Brother Bengt wrote some eighty letters to various pastors, inviting them to come and fellowship with me and to hear the message of love and unity in the Body of Christ. Out of the eighty, sixty of the pastors responded. The other twenty, we were told, were out of town. When they returned, they were very disappointed that they had missed the ministers' fellowship. The love and unity among the Christian churches of all denominations was a great blessing.

God has promised:

> *Behold, how good and how pleasant it is for brethren to dwell together in unity! It is like the precious ointment upon the head, that ran down upon the beard,*

A Long-Anticipated Journey to Sweden

*even Aaron's beard: that went down to the skirts of
his garments.* Psalm 133:1-2

It was a blessing to see people of all walks and ages
fellowshipping with each other in the churches of Sweden. There was no segregation between the young and
the old, the married and the single. There were no cliques
among the church groups. Everybody came together as
one Body.

The youth of Sweden were so stirred in the love of
Jesus that they brought in hard-core punk rockers to hear
the Word of God. Many of them gave their lives to Christ
and were gloriously filled with the Holy Spirit.

The hunger in the hearts of these young people was
very strong. One fourteen-year-old youth drove a farm
tractor fifteen miles to attend our services. He had no
other transportation to reach the service, and he was so
desperate that he borrowed his friend's tractor. It could
be driven without a license, and thus he was able to make
his way to the meeting. His trip was the talk of the town,
and the whole church was blessed to hear his testimony.

Two weeks passed rapidly, and the hunger of the Scan-
dinavians was not quenched. As soon as I returned
home, I received a telephone call from Brother Bengt in
Sweden. He said many ministers were literally weeping
for not having had the privilege of my holding services
in their churches.

The Scandinavian people had been very skeptical of
the faith message and the prosperity teaching presented
by some who did not live it. When they saw someone
come into the country totally by faith and preach the
Word in the pure love of Jesus, it attracted them.

137

Led by the Master's Hand

My ministry in Sweden is not complete, even though I have been there four different times. Much more must be done in Scandinavia. My prayer is that God would lead me there again in His perfect time.

CHAPTER 16

REACHING THE MILLIONS THROUGH THE YOUNGER GENERATION

He that believeth on me, the works that I do shall he do also; and greater works than these shall he do; because I go unto my Father. John 14:12

Although I am thrilled with what God has done and continues to do through my life, He has given me a great burden to challenge the younger generation to pick up the mantle and carry on. I can sense that God is ready to equip thousands of young warriors to do exploits for His Kingdom.

My personal goal has been, and still is, to win at least a million souls for Christ before I leave this world or before Christ returns. Many men have been led to prophesy over me that God would raise a younger generation through the latter part of my ministry and that this new generation would have a double portion of the anointing to win, not just one million, but millions upon millions.

When the Lord began to place this vision in my heart, I set about to pray for His guidance and wisdom, so that I could train many young men and women for world-wide evangelism.

In June of 1990, the Lord birthed in my heart a desire to raise up intercessors throughout the world to stand before His throne on behalf of worldwide evangelism. We started at home, in Scottsdale, Arizona, and our intention was to start intercessory groups throughout Indonesia, Malaysia, Singapore, India and any other country the Lord would indicate. We were sure that as the believers of each nation would travail in the Spirit before God for deliverance for their respective countries, the Lord would hear their prayers and bring forth a great deliverance, just as He had done for the children of Israel in delivering them from the land of Egypt. Their deliverance is a type of freedom from sin.

India, for instance, my native land, has been under the bondage of sin, sickness and poverty for more than four thousand years. It is time that the Christians of India learned to travail in the Spirit and pray for the deliverance of their nation. In every nation of the world, Christians need to groan and weep before God for the salvation of their countrymen. For this very cause, we intended to train young men and women to intercede for worldwide evangelism.

My burden for India was to raise up effective national evangelists, equipped with the power of the Holy Spirit to reach the unreached masses throughout their nation. Of the nine hundred million people in the country, only three percent are Christians. Many millions in the tribal areas had never heard the Gospel of Jesus Christ even once. It seemed so unreasonable that some hear the Gospel over and over, while others have not yet heard it.

We have planned a national evangelism training center in Madras to train and equip national evangelists. These evangelists would be given training in the Scriptures and the full-Gospel deliverance ministry. As they proved faithful in their ministry, they would be supported from our Worldwide Harvester Center headquarters in Scottsdale, Arizona. Each evangelist would have a bicycle to travel into remote areas and villages to present the Gospel through distributing tracts and preaching the Word of God. These men would also be trained to live by faith and to learn to trust in God, rather than looking to the West or to the East for support. The training center would be built and operated totally by faith, as a faith testimony to the young evangelists who would attend:

> *Now the just shall live by faith: but if any man draw back, my soul shall have no pleasure in him.*
>
> Hebrews 10:38

> *For as many as are led by the Spirit of God, they are the sons of God.*　　　　　Romans 8:14

And this is not the end of the vision. God continues to place nations and peoples within our hearts, and we continue to respond to Him and to see His miracles performed. It is my prayer that each and every one who reads this book will purpose to be *Led by the Master's*

141

Hand. May the Lord richly bless you as you launch out into a deeper walk of faith and prayer with God, to glorify Him and be His witness.

Amen!

Coming soon!

Led by the Master's Hand, Part II

If you were thrilled and challenged by the accounts of this book, look for the continuation of the faith-building account of the life and ministry of Missionary Evangelist Charles W. Doss. The author will thrill you with:

- Adventures of faith missionary stories from around the world

- His miraculous entry into some of the most hostile nations of the Earth for evangelism

- Notable miracles of healing

- God's faithfulness in providing every need

Ministry address:

Worldwide Harvester Center, Inc.
PO Box 2066
Scottsdale, Arizona 85252
USA

Additional copies of this and other books by Dr. Charles Doss may be ordered from your favorite bookstore or directly from the above address.